I WANT TO LIVE LIKE A PRINCE— ON A PAUPER'S BUDGET!

Impossible? **Money** magazine says it can be done—if you have the facts. DOLLAR PINCHING gives you all the information you need, with comprehensive, proven strategies that will dramatically shave your annual expenses and allow you to put more of your money to work. Now get the answers to your most important money-saving questions:

• How can I cut my kids' college bills by 40 percent?
• What kind of mortgage should I have?
• How can I negotiate a better price on my next car?
• How can I find a low-priced vacation package?

Dollar Pinching

Money® magazine

An Alternate Selection of **Money** Book Club™, Book-of-the-Month Club®, and Quality Paperback Book Club®

Other books in the
Money® America's Financial Advisor series:

How to Retire Young and Rich

401(k) Take Charge of Your Life

Paying for Your Child's College Education

The Right Way to Invest in Mutual Funds

Dollar Pinching

A Consumer's Guide to Smart Spending

Shelly Branch

WARNER BOOKS

A Time Warner Company

A NOTE FROM THE PUBLISHER

This publication is designed to provide competent and reliable information regarding the subject matter covered. However, it is sold with the understanding that the author and publisher are not engaged in rendering legal, financial, or other professional advice. Laws and practices often vary from state to state and if legal or other expert assistance is required, the services of a professional should be sought. The author and publisher specifically disclaim any liability that is incurred from the use or application of the contents of this book.

Warner Books, Inc., 1271 Avenue of the Americas, New York, NY 10020
Visit our Web site at
http://pathfinder.com/twep

 A Time Warner Company

Printed in the United States of America
First Printing: January 1997
10 9 8 7 6 5 4 3

Library of Congress Cataloging-in-Publication Data
Branch, Shelly.
    Dollar pinching : a consumer's guide to smart spending / Shelly Branch.
        p. cm.
    Includes index.
    ISBN 0-446-67246-7
    1. Consumer education—United States. 2. Finance, Personal—United States. I. Title.
TX336.B73 1997
640'.42—dc20   96-38402
                                                        CIP

Book design and composition by L&G McRee
Cover design by Bernadette Evangelist © 1996 by Robert Anthony, Inc.
Cover illustration by Peter Hoey

ACKNOWLEDGMENTS

My deepest appreciation to all the folks who, during the course of this project, generously shared their expertise and trade secrets. I'd especially like to thank Ruth Susswein at BankCard Holders of America; James Bragg at Fighting Chance; Mary Lou Andre at Organization by Design; Ron Rogé from the National Association of Personal Financial Advisors; Keith Gumbinger at HSH Associates; Charles Inlander at the People's Medical Society; Jean Salvatore at the Insurance Information Institute; John Markese from the American Association of Individual Investors; Randy Peterson at *InsideFlyer;* Tom Parson from *Best Fares;* Ashley Napp at AudoAdvisor; Richard Nigosian at Bond Street Travel; Tom Julian from the Men's Fashion Institute; Ken Goldstein from the Conference Board; Chris Christensen at the American Homeowners Foundation; and Steve Loucks from the American Society of Travel Agents.

Thanks also to **MONEY** magazine's Rich Eisenberg and Frank Lalli; my Warner editor, Rick Wolff; and, of course, all my family and friends who helped keep up my spirits all those late nights.

The final nod, of course, must go to my talented colleagues at **MONEY** magazine—especially Brian Clark, Elizabeth Fenner, Genevieve Fernandez, Jeanhee Kim, Leslie Marable, and Anamaria Wilson. Without their hard work and inspiration this book would not have been possible.

CONTENTS

INTRODUCTION

A Tribute to the Consumer's Might (and Plight)

Who drives the U.S. economy? If you think the answer is big business, or maybe even government, guess again. Consumers—everyday spenders just like you—power the nation's money engine.

Each year, hard-charging Americans shell out roughly $4.6 trillion on everything from cars and homes to clothing and vacations. That's a stunning *two-thirds* of the country's gross domestic product. Unfortunately, though, consumers don't always get the most mileage from those high-octane spending sprees. We overpay for many goods and services. Or we skimp on others that could save us dollars in the long term. Worst of all, we're digging ourselves into a den of debt, just to stay afloat. Debt, of course, is that consumer's catch-22. Sure, credit cards and installment loans enable us to acquire more stuff—real-life necessities like new homes and educations. But too much debt hampers our ability to *save* and *invest*—two regimens central to achieving the proverbial American dream.

That's where this book comes in. On the following pages we'll show you how to make your every dollar count, whether you're shopping for a home or a low-rate credit card. Don't confuse *Dollar Pinching,* by the way, with other authors' attempts to tidy up your budget. We won't waste your time by advising you to save soap scraps. And we never equate savings with sacrifice (trading down from a hotel room, for instance, to a tent). Rather, the idea behind *Dollar Pinching* is to save you big bucks comfortably, in the areas where they truly count, like buying a home, a car, health insurance, a vacation, and more. The end result: a leaner budget that will free up more money for long-term goals like retirement and maybe trading up to a larger home.

Dollar Pinching, we should mention, is the fifth entry in the **MONEY:** *America's Financial Advisor* series of personal finance books. Its counterparts offer superb advice on investing, retirement, and building a solid 401(k). If you fear you're light-years away from even tackling those goals, then this book is the best place to start. Why? Because the dollars you'll save—by using your negotiating leverage with banks and unleashing our black-belt techniques at the car dealership—will give your budget the lift it needs to make those other goals gradually fall into place.

But before you start obsessing over *how* to save, you probably want to assess *where* you need to save most. Enter the monthly budget, the jumping-off point recommended by all good financial planners. If you haven't done so already, you may want to sit down and draft a real-life monthly budget, factoring in your fixed expenses (such as housing costs and taxes) and estimating variable expenses (clothing, entertainment, health care). To get started, you don't necessarily need fancy spreadsheets or computer programs. As one financial planner recommends, you might simply clip a small piece of paper to your wallet and record every single dollar you spend. At week's end, compare your actual spending to the budget you've written in advance. Track your "income" and "outgo" for several weeks to find your vulnerable spots. Did you blow your targets for clothing, home furnishings, or medical costs? You may be surprised by the results, but you can improve them: Rethink your priorities. Try not to load up on additional debt. And read this book.

One last note: *Dollar Pinching* isn't just the name of this book. It's an acquired set of skills. Some of the best coups, in fact, can be scored by sheer improvisation. Just ask my dad. When I applied to Barnard College back in 1982, my application for financial aid came back with a disappointingly low offer—not the sort of response my parents had hoped for. With the quiet resolve of Gandhi, Dad planted himself outside the financial aid director's office, where he managed to persistently plead our case for nearly two weeks. Each visit, my father drove 20 miles there and back. The director's dog growled at him every time. But wouldn't you know it? The officers finally broke, coming up with a package worth over $3,000 for each of my four years. So with a bit of effort, my family saved $12,000. And, thankfully, Dad never got bit.

CHAPTER 1

Reap Mansion-Size Savings When You Buy or Sell Your Home

If you haven't already staked out a patch of real estate, it's likely that a home—complete with a lawn, automatic garage-door opener, and yes, meddlesome neighbors—is your biggest object of desire. Affording more than just shelter, however, a home of one's own opens the door for myriad tax savings. Specifically, homeowners get to bask in the tax deductibility of both mortgage interest and property taxes. Stay put long enough, and your castle will likely reward you further with price appreciation and equity. You can harness that equity buildup to help fund many of life's major expenses, such as college tuition, retirement, or even a new car. And if after age 55 you decide to sell, Uncle Sam allows you to pocket up to $125,000 of any profits, tax-free.

Your brick or wooden fortress, though, is hardly the rocket-like investment of a decade ago, when 10%-a-year house-value jumps weren't uncommon. Today's average home, priced at about $114,000, is likely to just keep up with inflation, appreciating at a rate of about 3% a year. Moreover, the real estate market isn't as accommodating as Wall Street, where investors choose when to buy in and when to bail out. Owners may be forced to sell in a down market, losing thousands; and buyers can get stuck with vertigo-inducing prices and/or mortgage rates. Bottom line: Whether you're looking to move in or out, you'll need an attic full of tips on how to lower your costs.

When It Pays to Own vs. Rent

First things first. Does it make sense for you to buy a home? Or should you rent into oblivion? After all, you can't beat the convenience of leasing. Finicky boilers and ravenous termites are the landlord's worry, not yours. On the other hand, there are weightier issues to consider, like *timing*. On average, homeowners stay put for a period of seven years. If you plan to move before that, renting may be the cheaper alternative. Why? Because it typically takes years to recoup the costs associated with buying a home. These include loan fees, agent fees, closing fees, and the like. You may also suffer the double punch of modest house price appreciation and high selling expenses.

If rents in your area are amazingly cheap, then that's good cause to consider sticking with a lease. Generally, if you could lease comparable digs for *65% or less* of the amount you'd pay to own—including your mortgage, taxes, and insurance—renting is worth a look, at least for a few years. Over the long term, however, homeownership rules. Having a fixed-rate mortgage, and all of the tax perks that come with it, is far preferable to rising rents over a 10- to 20-year stretch.

The following table highlights some of the most affordable housing markets in the United States. If your area is among the bunch, and you still rent, some low-key browsing may be in order.

TEN CITIES WHERE IT'S WISE TO BUY

According to E&Y Kenneth Leventhal Real Estate Group, a national consulting firm, the housing markets listed below are among the ripest in the nation for homeownership. Affordability in these regions is largely the result of modest home price appreciation and below average mortgage costs.

Metropolitan-Area	Ownership Cost (on average, as a % of income)
1. Oklahoma City	19.5%
2. Kansas City, Mo.	20.9%
3. Houston	21.4%
4. Tulsa	21.4%
5. St. Louis	22.0%
6. Central New Jersey	22.0%
7. Grand Rapids	22.2%
8. Salt Lake City	22.4%
9. Dallas/Fort Worth	22.6%
10. Louisville	22.7%

Money-Saving Mortgage Smarts

Today's standard home mortgage has a six-digit balance and carries a glacierlike term of 30 years. That sort of commitment is scary enough on its own. But what most people don't readily understand is the jaw-dropping math behind such loans. Take, for instance, a fixed-rate $100,000 mortgage at 8%. What would you imagine to be your total costs over that three-decade period? If you guessed $108,000, sorry—you're way off base.

Even a wager of $180,000 is far from the mark. After 30 years of interest payments, plus closing costs, inspection charges, points, and other niggly fees, *that $100,000 loan costs you just over $264,000.* Before you grab the Tums, relax. There are plenty of cost-conscious ways to make homeownership less painful.

SPOT THE MORTGAGE THAT'S RIGHT FOR YOUR NEEDS

Today's mortgage landscape features a beguiling array of products: the traditional 30-year fixed-rate loan, a one-year adjustable-rate mortgage (ARM), hybrid loans like the so-called 10/1 ARM—even one that's hyped as a combo annuity and mortgage. As you might imagine, finding the leanest mortgage among the bunch is no easy task.

Before you go dragging out your spreadsheets, though, consider some basics. Generally, you must choose between a mortgage with *fixed* or *variable* payments. With the fixed-rate variety, your monthly notes won't ever budge. Payments on variable, or adjustable-rate, mortgages, on the other hand, will fluctuate with interest rates. Which one stands to be easiest on your family finances? The answer depends on your monthly budget, the direction interest rates are heading, and how long you plan to stay in your home.

If you plan on taking up residence indefinitely, and mortgage rates are bobbing below 10%, a fixed rate is probably your best deal for long-term savings. Even though newspapers sound alarm bells when fixed rates rise from 7% to 8%, anything below 10% is still historically low and therefore attractive. In these conditions, it's usually not worth exposing yourself to the inevitable rate hikes of an adjustable loan, which can increase the interest rate by up to two percentage points a year (to a maximum of six points over the loan's term).

For restless types who plan to sell or refinance in three to five years, an adjustable-rate mortgage can tote up the bigger savings.

Generally, rates on a traditional one-year ARM are rock bottom for the first 12 months; thereafter they adjust with government bond rates. (Again, typical maximum increases are two points per year, with a six-point cap.) Recently, for example, borrowers paid an initial rate of 5.8% for a one-year ARM. A 30-year fixed rate, on the other hand, went for 8.25%. A one-year ARM can be an especially smart choice if you suspect that interest rates will be headed south at some point in the near future. Before you scoop up an ARM, however, remember this cardinal rule: *Rates on a one-year ARM should be a full two points below fixed rates to merit your attention.* Otherwise the fixed loan is likely the better deal.

If you plan to stay in your home between five and 10 years, then a so-called multiyear ARM may actually be cheaper than the previous options. A hybrid of sorts, this type of loan starts out with a fixed rate lasting for three, five, seven, or 10 years. After that, rates adjust much like a regular one-year ARM. The result, for many homeowners, is the best of both mortgage worlds. Takers get the low initial rate of an adjustable loan, combined with the stability of a fixed-rate product. By going for a 3/1 ARM, for instance, you'd enjoy three solid years of fixed payments before the loan converts. The same applies to a 5/1 or a 7/1 ARM, where your fixed payments will last, respectively, for five or seven years.

The best part: The average homeowner moves or refinances within seven years, so borrowers may never have to fuss with those costly adjustable rates. Rates for these loans fall somewhere between a one-year ARM and a 30-year fixed, with a 3/1 carrying the lowest and a 10/1 the highest.

PINCHING TIP

Loan schedules are tricky formulas that even banks have been known to screw up. Because ARM rates, in particular, gyrate up and down, the chances for error are bigger than you might think. If you decide to go with an ARM, you can get a free audit offered by the American Homeowners Foundation. It just might win you a cash refund. According to the foundation, about 7% of the loans they review contain costly errors. Recently the outfit recorded two major overcharges, of $14,000 and $10,000 each. The service won't cost you anything up front. But if a refund is due, you split the spoils 50-50. To find out more about the RE-ARM program, contact the foundation at 6776 Little Falls Rd., Arlington, Va. 22213-1213, or phone 703-536-7776.

FIND THE MORTGAGE LENDER WITH THE BEST DEAL

Stumble on your homework here, and you'll get a dunce cap that could cost you thousands of dollars in interest payments. Remember, lenders compete heavily for mortgage loans, so don't just scoot over to your local bank. One institution featured recently in **MONEY** magazine, for instance, was charging 5% less than the national average fixed rate of 8.81% at the time. While such a discrepancy might not sound so significant, the long-term impact is substantial. Over a 30-year period, assuming a fixed-rate mortgage of $150,000, the low-rate borrower comes out $20,000 ahead of the person who settled for the average rate. So compare, compare, compare.

To get the best mortgage mileage, you need to stack up more than just interest rates, however. The other part of the mortgage equation features *points*. Points are banking lingo for prepaid interest. A mortgage may carry anywhere from zero to three points (each point represents 1% of the loan amount; hence one point on a $100,000 loan costs $1,000). In exchange for a lower rate, and lower monthly payments, many lenders will pile more points onto your loan. That's not always such a good deal. Interest costs on an 8% mortgage with no points can come out cheaper than a 7.6% mortgage with two points, depending on how long you stay in your home.

To size up which is the better deal—a lower rate with more points, or fewer points with a higher rate—ask at least three lenders to run the numbers for you, factoring in total interest costs, closing costs, and any up-front charges such as calculations for you. Which will cost you less in the long run if you're in your home for three, five, or 10 years? To simplify things, you can consider this general rule of thumb: Buyers who plan to stay in their homes for four years or less are generally better off with a higher rate and fewer points; those who plan to retire in their castles should go for the lower rate and more points.

Now, back to logistics. You'll have many places to shop for what's surely the biggest debt of your life. Once again, don't run to your bank. Shop there, but begin a solid rate search by using data from **MONEY** magazine, your local newspaper, and/or HSH Associates. For a fee of $20, Butler, N.J.–based HSH will supply you with its *Homebuyer's Mortgage Kit,* containing mortgage rates on most lenders in your area. The kit also includes a mortgage shopping primer. Write to HSH at 1200 Rte. 23, Butler, N.J. 07405, or call 800-873-2837.

What if you've got spotty credit, a checkered career, or an erratic salary that makes lenders nervous? A reputable *mortgage broker* can help finesse any of these problems and save less-than-perfect borrowers thousands of dollars in the process. Until recently, the nation's 19,000 mortgage brokers were regarded as little more than pawnbrokers in the real estate market. Today, these professionals arrange roughly half of all home loans written each year. Their trade: securing wholesale-rate loans from banks and other lenders, then passing on some of the savings to borrowers like you.

Even if you do go with a mortgage broker, you should still check rates and fees at half a dozen local banks. You want to be certain you're getting the best possible terms. And if your broker requests pesky up-front fees, turn tail. Most require only a credit check fee (about $50) and a standard appraisal fee of $200–$300. For a list of mortgage brokers in your area, write the National Association of Mortgage Brokers, 8201 Greensboro Drive, Street 300, McLean, VA, 22102.

Aside from banks, thrifts, and mortgage brokers, several other mortgage lenders are worth checking out. If you belong to a *credit union*, or have access to one, be sure to check out their home loan offerings. Also, employees at large corporations may find *company grants* for down payments, or help with closing costs. (Schedule a visit with your benefits counselor to explore the opportunities.)

PINCHING TIP

Everything's negotiable, from mortgage rates to all the costs associated with closing the deal. These include points, attorney's fees ($200), "processing" fees ($150–$250), and even appraisal fees ($300). If you've done business with your lender in the past, you may be entitled to some breaks on these fees.

PINCHING TIP

To protect yourself in the event that rates increase after you've committed to a mortgage, get your lender to lock in your rate for 60 or 90 days. Most borrowers need that much time to settle on a home and close the deal.

MAKE THE LARGEST—NOT THE SMALLEST—DOWN PAYMENT YOU CAN

Most lenders require a standard 10% or 20% home down payment, a hurdle many first-time home buyers can't clear. Several mortgage programs, however, grease the wheels of homeownership by letting first-time borrowers put as little as 3% down. These are often associated with the Federal National Mortgage Association (Fannie Mae) and the Federal Housing Administration (FHA). While these types of loans make it easier for more people to qualify for a mortgage, and keep monthly payments manageable, *they are not for dollar pinchers.* Why? Because a lean down payment guarantees two miseries: higher interest costs and a need for private mortgage insurance. That last little treat, known as PMI, is required by most lenders for borrowers who pledge less than 20% down. Annoyingly, PMI effectively raises the roof on your interest rate by about one-quarter of a point.

Raising your down payment, on the other hand, will lower your total interest costs dramatically. On a $100,000 loan at 8.25%, for instance, borrowers who put down 20% can save a whopping $9,3000—in just ten years—over those who put down 10%.

(As a footnote, contrarian wisdom says that it's best to take out the biggest mortgage amount possible and invest your monthly savings to reap maximum returns. That's a fine theory—and one that can work if you've got the discipline, and the knack, to plow those funds into well-chosen, tax-friendly investments. The reality check here: Most people don't.)

CONSIDER THE MANSION-SIZE SAVINGS OF A 15-YEAR MORTGAGE

Maybe just the thought of a 30-year mortgage makes you cringe. If you're able to shell out an extra 20% or so on your monthly mortgage note, a 15-year fixed-rate mortgage can save you both anxiety and money. Rates on these abbreviated loans average about one quarter point less than 30-year obligations. *Even better, by halving your payback time, the average homeowner can save almost $100,000 in interest costs.*

Hard to believe? Consider the following example. On a 30-year $100,000 fixed-rate loan at 8%, monthly notes come to about $734. After 30 years, or 360 payments, the amount paid in interest only is a roof-raising $164,155. Compare that with a 15-year loan, which might carry a rate of 7.75%. Monthly payments are higher, at $941, but after 180 notes, your interest costs ring in at $69,430—a savings of nearly $95,000.

Another perk: A 15-year mortgage gives borrowers an equity edge. By paying off the loan interest and principal more quickly, you accumulate equity twice as fast—boosting your prospects to profit from a future sale.

SNARE YOUR HOUSE BARGAIN FAST WITH A PREAPPROVED MORTGAGE

As its name implies, a preapproved mortgage secures your cash before you even go shopping, a neat idea that carries several money-saving advantages. Chief among them is *negotiating leverage.* In the typical real estate transaction, the lengthiest process is getting the financing in order. A written commitment from a lender, stating your approved mortgage amount and rate, shows sellers that you can close the deal—pronto. Such ready money may be all it takes to nudge their asking price a few grand south. Preapproval gives you another, more personal edge.

It encourages budget control. You're far less likely to fall in love with Southfork when a lender approves you for mere hillbilly digs.

PINCHING TIP

There's nothing like a preapproved mortgage (ready money) to put sellers in a favorable negotiating mood. Just don't confuse this type of written commitment with a mortgage "prequalification." Virtually anybody can get the latter, which is merely a note from a lender stating the amount you can afford to borrow. Beyond that, it offers no guarantees.

BUY ONLY AS MUCH HOUSE AS YOU NEED

You'll want to be starkly realistic about how grand a home you can afford to buy. Trust us: better to err on the low side than be saddled with a place you can't maintain, or one that saps your resources to the point of discomfort. As a rule, try to limit your search to houses costing no more than *three times your gross annual salary.* Your total monthly housing costs, including mortgage payments, insurance, and property taxes, should not zoom past 30% of your gross income. One way to discipline yourself: Prior to shopping, prepare a list of home characteristics you must have, plus another list of traits you simply don't need.

KNOW WHEN TO GO HOUSE HUNTING

With housing market and interest rate fluctuations, it's anybody's guess as to the best year or month to buy. History shows us that house shoppers can find the most welcome mats during the months of October, November, and December. Though it's unlikely you'll find an abundance of homes up for sale during the holiday season, sellers during these busy months are usually anxious and willing to lower their prices. Try not to freeze your plans until January; historical sales data indicate that the first month of the year is also the costliest for home buyers.

LOOK FOR THE BEST LOCAL DEALS

Sellers with homes fresh on the market tend to be the most optimistic. That's old hat in the real estate business, where prices start out high, then come back down to reality as the months trickle by. To increase your chances of getting the best initial price on a home, ask real estate agents to steer you to homes whose sellers have recently dropped their asking prices by 3% to 5%.

SHOP FOR A HOME THAT'S "FOR SALE BY OWNER"

In some housing markets, you may find owners willing to sell themselves without the aid of a real estate broker. Known affectionately in real estate slang as FIZBO, this sales strategy is a boost for both the seller (who saves on realty fees) and the buyer, too. How? By leaving brokers out of the equation, a FIZBO seller may have more leeway on price, giving you more wiggle room in negotiations.

USE A BUYER'S BROKER

Usually, brokers work in force for home sellers. However, hiring a similar advocate to work on your side can shave about 5% off the purchase price of a home. A buyer's broker is for hire at most any real estate office, only in this case he or she works exclusively with you, the house shopper. They will coach you on property values and market activities in your vicinity and brainstorm to come up with the shrewdest bids. Hopefully their smarts will result in a lower purchase price than you could've achieved on your own. In the best-case scenario, you'll still save 4%–5% after subtracting the broker's fee—typically 3% or so of the house price.

NEGOTIATE THE HOUSE PRICE

Of course, you want to land the best deal possible. Just how well you do depends on two factors: timing and tenacity. The first you can do little about, since buyers are at the mercy of local real estate markets. The stronger the market in your area—if homes are selling swiftly for close to their asking prices—the slimmer your chances for hammering out a great deal. Some folks may even consider postponing a home purchase or looking in a different region to snare a better bargain.

Start by assessing the asking price. Is it fair? You can discern this pretty quickly by browsing local newspaper ads for similar homes and chatting up several local brokers about market conditions in general. (Most will be happy to supply you with a handy price analysis of homes recently sold in the area.) Next, look at the sellers. How anxious are they to unload their home? They may be moving on a new home contract themselves and willing to lower the price if the timing is right. Finally, keep your cool. Appearing overly eager to a seller will surely diminish your negotiating powers.

As a benchmark, aim to knock at least 5% off the seller's price. (Of course, this assumes that the real estate climate is right for negotiations of any kind. If you're buying in a "hot" market, where homes move swiftly, prepare yourself to offer a seller's asking price or more.)

Rather than dwell on price, price, price, put a creative spin on your negotiations. Are there furnishings in the home that the seller is willing to leave behind if you agree to his counteroffer? Is the seller willing to share in closing costs such as attorney's fees? You might also ask that the seller pay part or all of your mortgage points. If they agree to do so, you win twice: points on a primary residence are fully deductible on your federal tax return, *even when paid by the seller.*

ORDER UP A HOME INSPECTION TO SAVE ON FUTURE HEADACHES

Scrimping on a $200–$300 home inspection—a series of engineering checks to assure a place's physical soundness—simply doesn't pay. What appears to be a minor ceiling leak, for instance, could be the beginnings of serious roof decay. For about $250 you can get a written inspection of your dream home's structure. Any defects uncovered by the inspector can be grounds for negotiating your price south (although you may need to make the repairs yourself). Be sure to ask your real estate agent for referrals to a reputable home inspector, since the field is crowded with shysters.

Three Ways Homeowners Can Reap Ongoing Savings

PREPAY YOUR MORTGAGE

Maybe those savings sound delicious, but you just can't swing the higher monthly payments. Another way to drain big dollars from your mortgage is to prepay the balance. No, you won't have to hand over a check for 50 grand. On the contrary, you can tame your debt substantially by adding just a dollop more to your monthly mortgage tab.

Let's assume, using that same 30-year loan just described, that you can afford to pay an extra $25 on your monthly note. This increases your $734 payment to $759. By doing so, you will not only reduce your payback time from 30 to 26 years, you will also save the satisfying sum of roughly $23,000 over the course of the loan.

Now, before you race to write that next mortgage check, find out if your lender charges a prepayment penalty. That's the punishment banks and other institutions charge for docking their profits in the first few years of your mortgage. If you're slapped with such a penalty, ask to have it waived. Even better, ask prospective lenders, *before you sign*, whether your mortgage would carry such penalties.

MAKE BIWEEKLY PAYMENTS

There's yet another way to save handsomely on your mortgage costs without adding any extra dollars. Impossible, you say? Not at all. Take our same 30-year obligation, at $734 per note, and split it in two. Literally. Rather than mail one check every month, plan to mail a check every two weeks, for a payment of $367 each time. It's a simple accounting trick, but a valuable one nevertheless. By using such a schedule, *you'll cut your mortgage term by about seven years, saving nearly $46,000 in the process.* Actually, there's a simple explanation for the savings. Because most months are longer than four weeks, the biweekly schedule forces you to make 26 payments per year, speeding up your payback time by one full month each year.

KNOW WHEN IT PAYS TO REFINANCE

The minute that interest rates take a tumble, your mortgage may begin to look shabby. Suddenly, signs for "refinancing" appear in every bank window and advertisement. And indeed, swapping your old rate for a leaner new one probably holds big appeal. But will refinancing automatically yield savings? Not necessarily, so you must know how to size up the deal.

Start by canvassing rates—again. Your current lender may not have the best deal. In fact, refinancing your mortgage won't be too different from your first application process. Points and closing fees and credit checks will come to haunt you, as well as title insurance and other expenses. Add up these costs one by one. (On a $150,000 30-year loan at 7%, for instance, they might total $4,000.) Next ask your lender to project your new monthly payment. This note will surely be lower than the old one, but now you must factor in those refinancing costs— $4,000 as mentioned above. How long will it take you to come out ahead or to recoup that $4,000 with the new loan? Generally, at least two to three years. In the case just cited, assuming your payments slide from $1,153 a month at 8.5% to $998 at $8.5%, it would take 26 months to break even. If you plan to stay in your home for at least that long, or preferably a few years longer, refinancing is a smart move.

PINCHING TIP

When you go to refinance a 30-year fixed-rate mortgage, consider refinancing with a 15-year loan, as previously outlined. Your monthly payments may remain about the same, roughly. But you'll cut your payback time in half and reap fabulous interest savings.

Smart Pinching Strategies for Home Sellers

A new job calls you to Cleveland. A new baby is due at the end of the year. Maybe you simply hate your current house; or, happily, you want to pocket the profits of a soaring housing market. Whatever the case, you'll want to keep as much of your selling price in your pocket as possible. You'll be successful if you consider the following tips.

FORGET BROKERS AND SELL YOURSELF

Lots of folks may admire your castle. But no one covets your home more than a broker. And who can blame them? The average commission from a house sale is a healthy 6%. That's $8,400 on a home going for $140,000. If you're putting your house up on the block, the thought has probably occurred to you: Could I save a few grand by selling it myself? Though the vast majority—70%—of all homes are auctioned off by brokers, there's nothing to stop you from going counterculture. In fact, the number of owners who sell themselves has risen 10% in the past five years.

The best candidates for selling their own homes are energetic types who won't mind fielding calls and visits from both browsers and serious shoppers alike. The do-it-yourself route works even better for owners whose homes are in pristine condition and would likely sell quickly anyway.

Of course, there are some costs associated with selling yourself. Figure on spending about $200 on advertising and upkeep for every month your place is on the market. That's still an extra $8,000 in your pocket if your $140,000 home sells in two months—a real boon for homeowners with scant equity. Or look at it another way. Without a commission to pay, you can probably afford to price your home slightly lower than competing houses in the neighborhood—a sure way to score bids in a tough market.

Should you decide to wear your own broker's hat, don't neglect hiring a lawyer to shepherd you through all contract negotiations. Visual types might even profit from a 67-minute video on going it alone. *How to Sell Your Own Home* is produced by Vermont-based Picket Fences, a publisher of home-sale directories. To order your copy ($19.95) call the publisher toll-free at 800-489-7776.

IF YOU'RE IN A HOT HOUSING MARKET, TRY A DISCOUNT REAL ESTATE BROKER

As mentioned above, a broker typically takes 6% of your home's selling price as his or her fee. This is money out of your pocket (though you may convince a seller to share in these costs) and that pays for marketing costs and the broker's time. Assuming you lack the time and energy to sell yourself, but don't quite need the firm push of a traditional broker, there's one good compromise: a discount broker. You'll find these semi-service pros in your Yellow Pages. Charging 2%–4%, or nearly half as much as their competitors, a cut-rate broker can save you thousands on a transaction. The question is, can you do without the full range of broker services? For instance, you'll lose the privilege of getting your home in the multiple listing service (MLS), through which brokers share information. However, a house in a spry market may not need the extra marketing push.

MAKE SURE THE PRICE IS RIGHT

Setting too high an asking price assures your house won't budge from the market. Even if you think you're being shrewd—you know, asking a high initial price, then "slashing" it—such tactics can easily backfire. Who wants a home that's languished, inexplicably, on the market? Or one that appears plain old unaffordable? Find the best target price by interviewing several real estate agents. Double-check their estimates by looking in the newspaper for the prices of similar homes. You may want to keep watch for several weeks before you put your home on the block, to get an accurate gauge about pricing in your area.

SPRUCE YOUR PLACE UP, BUT DO IT ON THE CHEAP

Remember, first impressions count. So before you fling your doors wide to brokers and buyers, get your house in the best shape possible. Forget new furnishings, floors, and other major projects. Aside from major repairs that must be fixed prior to the sale, let the new homeowners do their own tinkering. Instead, address the basics that any home shopper would notice.

Begin with those focal points, like windows and walls—they could always use a good cleaning. Bad wall surfaces might merit some plaster and a few coats of paint. Beyond that, small upgrades can add a little luxury to your home's appearance. Try sparkling new brass doorknobs, for instance, or install brighter lighting in key areas like kitchens and bathrooms. Orderly closets, dripless faucets, and a spray of fresh flowers in the den can all do wonders to augment your place's looks and marketability. Generally, these spruce-ups should cost you no more than a few hundred dollars.

IF ALL ELSE FAILS . . . RENT YOUR HOUSE TO POTENTIAL BUYERS

It's easy to become discouraged if your home doesn't move off the market as swiftly as you'd like. There's no need, however, for you to suffer a flat-out loss if you're set to move and your house has no takers. One solution: Rent the space. Not indiscriminately, but to lessors who might cozy up to the idea of eventually buying. After figuring a fair market rental rate, you might offer to credit 10% of the monthly rent toward your place's purchase price.

DON'T FORGET TO GRAB THE TAX BREAKS YOU'RE DUE

The IRS serves up two tax breaks to cushion the trauma of selling your home. Don't get the wrong idea: Uncle Sam wants his fair share of taxes on any capital gains your sale scores. Luckily, though, you won't necessarily be taxed on every cent's difference between the house's original price and its selling price. How's that? When you sell, the IRS lets you add improvement costs to your home's original purchase price, thereby decreasing your taxable gains.

Let's say that you paid $80,000 for your home 10 years ago. Now you're moving out, having sold the place for $100,000. Rather than owe taxes on $20,000—the difference between the purchase price and the selling price—you can owe significantly less by adding improvement costs to the equation. For instance, that $5,000 kitchen job, plus those $1,000 wood floors installed in the den, adds up to $6,000. These two improvements spike your purchase price from $80,000 to $86,000, decreasing your taxable gain from $20,000 to $14,000. This figure is known as your *adjusted cost basis*.

To figure yours, compile a list of all improvements you've

made to your home. These should not be confused with routine maintenance (like painting and cleaning). Rather, they are bigger jobs such as room additions, roof replacements, and air-conditioning installations. Should you have trouble deciphering improvements from routine upkeep costs, consult IRS Publication 523: *Selling Your Home*. You can get a copy by calling the IRS at 800-829-3676.

Last stop on the IRS line of tax treats for sellers: As we mentioned at the beginning of this chapter, homeowners over the age of 55 get to savor a onetime tax deduction. Assuming you fall in this age group, an IRS rule lets singles and couples claim a deduction on up to $125,000 worth of capital gains realized from the sale of a primary residence. Take note, however, that folks on their second or third marriage may get penalized here. Unfortunately for the Liz Taylors of the world, the IRS stipulates that if you or your spouse took this exemption in a previous marriage, neither one of you can claim it again.

PINCHING TIP

Don't neglect writing off those points each year if you refinance. Failing to deduct $2,000 in points robs homeowners of nearly $600, assuming a 28% bracket.

CYBERTIP

A free service on the World Wide Web helps prospective homeowners tinker with all the possibilities outlined here. The Personal Financenter (http://www.financenter.com) contains built-in calculators (!) to help you figure mortgage payments, calculate the costs of refinancing, and much more. Another place worth browsing is the HomeOwners Finance Center (http://www.homeowners.com), which serves as primer on various mortgage products and also provides current interest rates.

CHAPTER 2

Drive Away with the Best Car Buys

How to Save When You Buy or Lease a New or Used Car

Finally, you've succumbed to the slick ads. You're obsessed with the aroma of taut leather seats, the reassuring *ka-thunk* of a new car door slammed shut, even your boss's envy. . . .

Enter reality. Second to a home, an automobile is probably the biggest single purchase you'll ever make. And while buying a new car is a dreamy proposition in the think-about-it stage, few other investments prove as frustrating. Each year 15 million Americans fan out to the nation's 22,750 auto lots, hoping for a fair shake. But if you've so much as set foot in a dealership, you know that just as in Vegas, the odds are in the house's favor. Let's start with the fact that *one in seven car buyers don't realize that a car's price is negotiable.* And disturbingly, at least half of all car shoppers—specifically women and minorities—have been proved losers over white males in the quest for aboveboard treatment. Shuffling the deck even more, a dealer may push leasing, his own financing, and a trunkful of extras you simply don't need.

Such headaches help explain why buying a car truly is the great American shell game. You, however, need not be one of the industry's casualties. Solder together these pieces of advice, and we guarantee you a smoother ride off the lot.

What You Need to Know to Save Thousands on a New Car

"Why, that price is ridiculous!! I've got fifteen grand in my pocket— take it or leave it!" The babbling negotiator's rap is admirable. Saving scads of money on a new car, however, takes a lot more than hubris. To start, you'll need to hoard as many pearls of information as possible on a dealer's *markup* and *hidden profits*. (Repeat those terms three times, for we will return to them later in earnest.) Once you've assembled a cheat sheet of sorts— and gathered some specific data on the auto industry in general—you'll be ready to swagger your way onto dealer lots to ignite a fabulous deal.

Your newspaper's business pages are a good place to begin sleuthing. Are car sales up or down? Any particular models lagging in sales, high in demand? Is the Japanese yen weak or strong, and how might that affect the cost of their imports? The news factor can give you a general sense of how eager dealers may be to turn a deal. Continue rooting for clues by visiting a few car lots under low-pressure circumstances. Is the place bustling or quiet as a graveyard? Do you notice an overabundance of white Ford Taurus models? Common sense can move you far in the car-buying game, especially when combined with the following tactics:

DON'T CRASH YOUR CAR BUDGET

How much can you afford to pay for a new car? Maybe you've been thinking GMC but dreaming BMW. Get that devil off your shoulder by first figuring how much of a down payment you can afford. Three thousand? Five thousand? Your initial ante should drive your total car price, since *smart car shoppers aim to put a minimum of 20% down, financing the rest over a period of no more than four years.*

Too tight a squeeze, you say? Not when you consider how that nasty phenomenon called depreciation can rob a new car of *one-third its value* in a matter of months. By taking out a short-term loan (two to four years vs. the typical maximum of seven), you decrease the risk of being saddled with a car worth less than your outstanding loan balance.

Another bonus: A hefty down payment will endear you to lenders. Putting 20% or more down almost guarantees you a loan rate more favorable than 10%. This can dash your rate by a full percentage point or better at banks and credit unions. How much does that stand to put in your pocket? For every percentage point you knock off the APR, you'll save $20.50 for every $1,000 borrowed on a 48-month loan.

SAVE BY NAILING DOWN YOUR FINANCING FIRST

Get your car loan lined up before sailing onto dealer lots. Not only will this force you to commit to a budget, but preapproval on a car loan will almost surely yield you a better rate. (A hint: Don't let on to a dealer that you've cleared the money hurdle. Your willingness to look at his financing may ease the negotiations along.)

HOW A SHORT-TERM LOAN
SAVES YOU BIG TIME

	Monthly note at 8.00%*	Total interest payments
2-YEAR LOAN		
$15,000	$678	$1,282
$20,000	$905	$1,709
4-YEAR LOAN		
$15,000	$366	$2,577
$20,000	$488	$3,436
7-YEAR LOAN		
$15,000	$234	$4,369
$20,000	$312	$6,185

*For illustration purposes, this chart assumes the same rate on short- and longer-term loans. Rates for short-term loans will actually be lower, costing you even less money in the long run.

The nation's 13,000 *credit unions* routinely post the best deals on both new and used auto loans. Count on grabbing a loan that's at least a full percentage point lower than the offerings at your bank. (To locate a credit union you may be able to join, contact the Credit Union National Association at 800-358-5710.)

After credit unions, *banks* should be your next pit stop. Head first to your own bank and inquire as to their very best rate. Then call or visit at least six others to get the lowdown on competing terms in your area. If your bank's rates seem high, head to your branch manager and say so. As a regular customer, you should get him or her to match any lower bids (assuming you qualify) or shave at least a half percentage point off his walk-up rates. One way to lock up a better deal: Offer to have your payments deducted from your checking account automatically.

The third option, *dealer financing,* is a roll of the dice. All dealerships will push it, since *selling money, not just cars, is key to a dealer's profits.* The worst setup (though a common one) is a loan your dealer brokers through a bank. In such arrangements he's likely to charge a middleman's fee of one to three percentage points above the rate you'd pay by applying directly at the bank yourself.

This doesn't mean you can't get some excellent financing terms at the car shop. The secret lies in the source of the loan, with *deals direct from the manufacturer reigning supreme.* An example: In 1996 Ford was offering 4.9% 48-month financing on its Contour and Taurus models, or roughly half the rates at most lending institutions. The newsletter *CarDeals* prints dozens of such incentive programs each month ($7 per issue; 800-475-7283).

Finally, some homeowners may turn to a *home-equity loan* to finance their wheels. About 13% of all home-equity loans are tapped for this purpose. Generally, borrowers can take out up to 80% of the equity in their home and deduct the interest on loans of up to $100,000. Factoring in the tax advantage, then, a person in the 28% tax bracket taking out an 8.5% loan gets the equivalent of a 6.1% car loan. One major caveat: Should you fall behind in payments, you risk losing both your roof and your sunroof.

NEVER PAY STICKER

As mentioned earlier, one out of seven car shoppers regards a car's sticker price as nonnegotiable. You, of course, are among the other six who see that sticker as mere *opinion.* (There is only one exception to this rule: for hot-selling, trendy cars such as the Ford Explorer, you may be forced to pay sticker or close to it.)

To drive a car cost south, you'll need a few pieces of nifty information. One is what the dealer paid, known as *dealer invoice*. The other is the car's *markup*—that's the profit built into the sticker. From there you can pinpoint your offering, or *target price*. Unlike Scrooge, you want your dealer to make a decent profit; but generally, *for cars listing at $20,000 or less, buyers should aim for a target price of between $300 to $700 over dealer invoice.* Snazzier wheels, with stickers of $25,000 to $40,000, call for a target price of $500 to $2,000 over invoice.

Getting the vital stats you need is a cinch. Several general reference books, including *Car Buying Made Easy,* break down the numbers on most models. Such general reference books are a good starting point, but remember: we are talking about the ultimate shell game here, where prices and statistics change from week to week. Serious negotiators will want to obtain more up-to-date data. Two excellent sources:

Fighting Chance gets manufacturers' latest car cost information every two weeks. For $19.95 (plus $3 shipping and handling) their package includes a new analysis for the car brand you specify, recent dealer invoice and retail prices, and details on dealer's hidden profits (see pages 30–31). Call 800-288-1134; or go on-line on the Internet: http://www.fightingchance.com

Just the Facts ($14.95, from IntelliChoice; 800-227-2665) tells you all the basics you'll need to know about the dream machine you specify. Subscribers to America Online (Keyword: CARS) and CompuServe (GO AUTOMOBILES) can tap into screen after screen of the most recent car price information.

LEARN A CAR'S TOTAL OWNERSHIP COST

When buying a new car, savvy types seek more than low costs: they demand value as well. So try not to obsess over monthly payments. Granted, your total monthly outlay—car note, insurance, gas, etc.—is an integral part of your budget and a number worth brooding over. But trust us: your monthly car payment is only part of the equation in figuring your ride's true cost.

Instead, a car's *five-year ownership cost* is the number to watch. This big-picture figure predicts how much you will pay to both own and operate your vehicle. Factored into the sum are depreciation, insurance, repairs, and registration fees. Boiled together, these numbers can yield surprising results. For example, a $15,000 car, depending on the model, can very well cost more to own than a $16,000 or $17,000 car.

For clues about your car's total ownership cost, consult publications such as **MONEY** magazine and *Consumer Reports,* which break down this figure for most car models in their annual auto guides. Or, for a small fee of about $20, you can request an ArmChair Compare report from IntelliChoice (800-227-2665). This document, mailed to your home, totes up ownership costs and other financial fun facts on any two car models of your choice.

KNOW YOUR WAY AROUND THE REBATE BLOCK

Television and newspaper ads blare "rebates" of $500 to $1,500 on many car models. Generally this is cash you can take up front or use as part of a down payment. Keep in mind, just because a car is a big seller doesn't exempt it from carrying a nice rebate. For instance, in early 1996 Ford was giving rebates of $600 on its popular Taurus model. In some cases you may be offered a choice of a rebate or a special low interest rate of about 3% or 4%. *If offered a rebate or a low-interest deal, go for the rebate.* Assuming you take out a short-term loan of two to three years, you stand to save more money by taking the rebate over the cheap financing.

GET YOUR DEALER TO SHARE HIS HIDDEN PROFITS

Most car shoppers don't know it, but you can get additional rebates, so to speak, by tapping your dealer's pocket. What lurks there? A secret goldmine—factory-to-dealer cash that's over and above any profit they make directly from you. Remember, dealers wouldn't harvest these hidden pearls—worth $500 to $3,000—without your sale. So why shouldn't you share in the spoils? By uncovering all the nooks and crannies of a dealer's profit, you gain more negotiating steam.

The two biggies to chase are *dealer holdbacks* and *factory-to-dealer incentives*. The *dealer holdback* is—once again—a fine example of the car biz shell game. Essentially a low-grade accounting trick, these paybacks give dealers "credits" on vehicles they've already financed. Such perks can range from $500 to more than $1,000, depending on the vehicle (Volvo's holdback is a flat $800 per car). While your dealer isn't likely to part with his cherished holdback, the mere mention of it could well shock him into a more pliable negotiating position.

Don't expect your dealer to tell you about *factory-to-dealer incentives*, either. These top-secret rewards put cash in a dealer's coffers for every vehicle the dealer moves. Recently Acura was paying dealers incentives of $1,200 for every Integra model moved; and BMW was kicking back as much as $3,000 to dealers unloading cars in its BMW-3 series. Armed with this information, you'll make it difficult for a dealer to cry poverty—and may even get him to rebate at least some of that cash to you. You'll find the information you need about factory-to-dealer incentives in the monthly newsletter *CarDeals* (202-347-7283; $7 per issue), which also lists current rebates on dozens of car models.

BEWARE DEALER PAKS AND OTHER SHOWROOM MUGGINGS

Count on a salesman to tempt you with all sorts of options and gizmos. Pick and choose—and pay—at your own discretion. Just say no, however, to those extras lurking on the dealer's sticker. Known commonly as *dealer options,* or *dealer paks,* these are often frivolous add-ons you did not request. Standard examples include fabric protectants (basically a $100 upholstery treatment you can do yourself with a few $10 cans of Scotchgard); paint sealants (largely redundant to excellent paint technology); and rust-proofing packages (which may actually damage your car's electrical workings). Installed by the dealer, the markup on these items is astronomic—as much as 300%. Negotiate the price of paks down to zero, or demand a factory-fresh car without the frills.

Two other extras to avoid:

Credit life insurance. A policy that promises to continue your payments in the event you die. This horrible rip-off sucks in millions of car buyers a year, even though it pays out an average of just 38 cents for every premium dollar spent. So just say no.

Extended warranties. Brace yourself for the hard sell on these policies, which cover repairs after your factory warranty bows out. The idea is quaint, but in fact their price tags—anywhere from $500 to $2,000—make them bum deals. Because standard warranties last up to three or four years on most models, there's slim logic to funding a policy that won't kick in until the twenty-first century. As an alternative, fashion your own warranty of sorts by stashing a few hundred dollars in a top-yielding money-market fund.

What You Need to Know to Close the New Car Deal

Having decided on a model and a budget, and blessed with sage insight into most tricks of the trade, you're now ready to act. Take a few deep breaths. And never appear anxious. An overly zealous customer is dealer bait. Express flexibility on models, colors, and so on. Doing so will reinforce your take-it-or-leave-it attitude.

Remember, *timing counts.* Your bargaining mileage is apt to vary depending on the time of year or month when you purchase your car. The best times to buy and negotiate: the end of a model year or when dealers have bloated inventories and need to move cars. The worst times to buy: two to three months after a new model has been introduced (remember the Miata?), when marketing hype dampens your dickering power.

PLAY YOUR NEGOTIATING HAND LIKE A SYMPHONIC CONDUCTOR

As a routine, dealers plead poverty when negotiating a car's price. By summoning up all your newfound skills regarding holdback, factory-to-dealer incentives, etc., you can dead-end their poorhouse argument. So unleash them as needed. Best order for firing:

1. "I understand the invoice price is $15,000, or $1,000 below sticker. So let's really talk price."
2. "Hmmm . . . I'd like to close this deal as soon as possible, so how about cutting me in on half of your $3,000 factory-to-dealer cash on that BMW?"
3. "Oh yes, I understand you get a handsome dealer holdback. Anything more we can we do with the price on that score?"

GRAB A NO-FUSS DEAL BY PHONE OR FAX

Equipped with a trunkload of information on a car's cost, and all sources of a dealer's profit, you can order a car, in some cases, as easily as you might Chinese food. Prepare a form letter (or a phone script), and direct your offer to the sales manager or fleet manager at the dealership. Spell out that you

- are ready to buy *tomorrow*, if certain conditions are met.
- know such an order will save the dealer on sales commissions.
- are fully aware of the invoice vs. sticker price (citing both).
- expect the dealer to share some of his factory-to-dealer cash.
- have a set price you are willing to pay (specifying the amount over invoice).
- are flexible on colors, etc.
- are available to talk that business day by phone (and leave your numbers).

Voilà! You may not get instant success this way, but the folks at *Fighting Chance,* who get piles of customer feedback, report that this no-hassle car-buying technique has scored awesome deals for several buyers nationwide.

LET SOMEONE ELSE DO YOUR BIDDING

For those who'd rather wrestle a bull than haggle with a car dealer, help awaits. Charging fees ranging from $250 to $500, the nation's 30 or so car-buying services can relieve much of your stress by locating the rock-bottom price for the model of your dreams. If you wish, they can even arrange to have your car delivered to your door.

Fully one in four car dealers today has relationships with such services. The deals make sense both for them and for the auto manufacturers, since quickie sales save on manpower and marketing costs.

Choose your service carefully. Though several large retailers (such as Sam's Club of Wal-Mart and Price/Costco) have jumped into the car-buying pool, the deals they cut (generally about $500 off list prices) are no match for the veterans of the business. Three excellent services that will track down the best price and handle the details to closing are Seattle-based AutoAdvisors (800-326-1976); CarSource in Larkspur, Calif. (800-517-2277); and Cincinnati-based Automobile Consumer Services (800-223-4882). Expect to pay $250–$350 for factory orders and $300–$375 to locate vehicles in stock. If all you desire, on the other hand, is a fistful of competitive prices, a good bet is Car Bargains (800-475-7283), which for a flat $150 fee will send you five blind quotes from local dealers on the model of your choice.

DON'T MAKE YOUR USED-CAR "TRADE-IN" A "TRADE-OFF"

Dealer trade-ins are a hassle-free way to unload one car and get a rebate on another. The term "trade-in" itself isn't so bad; you merely want to avoid a "trade-off"—a bum deal for the sake of convenience. You may be surprised to learn that many dealers *make more money selling used cars than new ones.* They buy low and sell high—a practice that doesn't jibe with your desire to get the best offer for your old mount.

To pocket 20% more than the average new-car dealer bid, *sell yourself.* You can get a gauge of your car's present value by flipping through *Edmund's Used Car Prices* (about $7 at many newsstands; or *free* for Web browsers at www.edmunds.com), which lists average selling prices for hundreds of car models. Further hone your asking price by keeping abreast of "For Sale" ads in your local paper and getting quotes from several used-car lots.

When you do place your own ad, specify either no price or one that gives you good negotiating room. It may take you several weeks or more to close a deal, but surveys show that this method nets owners about 20% more than they'd get on an average trade-in.

Regardless of what we say, some folks will insist on following the trade-in route. If you're of such a mind, that's fine—*as long as you negotiate the deals separately.* Earlier we talked about car sales as the ultimate shell game, and this is a fine example of how it is played. Say a dealer offers you a generous-sounding $3,000 for your used car—much more than you think you'd get on your own. Chances are he or she has padded the invoice price of your new car to offset that sum, leaving you with no fine deal. So if you must insist on doing a trade, sell your car in one transaction, then buy the new wheels in another.

PINCHING TIP
Want a simple way to figure out which car models are crawling off dealer lots? Casually check out the manufacturing date on the doorjamb to see which cars have been hanging around the longest—these are more likely to get you the best deal.

How to Get the Lowest-Cost Lease

The maxim of car leasing is this: It's never as simple as it seems. Sure, that ad touting low monthly payments paints a rather straightforward picture, even an affordable one. But dig behind the real numbers, and . . . well, the deal becomes convoluted.

So before delving into the fractions and formulas of a long-term rental (plain language for car leasing), you'll want to ask: Is a lease really the best option for me? The answer may be "yes" if you crave a spanky new ride every three or four years, and you drive fewer than 15,000 miles a year. For those who steer their cars to the junkyard, however, leasing doesn't make much sense.

There are plenty of reasons for this. For starters, *as much as three out of every four dollars you pay on a lease finance depreciation.* In other words, you are paying for most of the car's rapidly declining value up front. Long-term leases of, say, five years offer the worst example. In many cases you could buy the car outright for the same money you paid to rent the car over the lease term. No extra cash required at lease end.

If you decide that leasing is still your calling, keep in mind that these contracts are negotiable. Here's what you'll need to know.

LOW LEASE PAYMENTS DO NOT A BARGAIN MAKE

Here's where dealer trickery begins. Lease payments are based on the fraction of the car's value during the time you lease it. Hence they are generally lower than a regular car note. No bargain there. To navigate the lease maze, then, you'll need to examine the terms of a lease with microscopic precision. The following terms will help you decipher the true cost over the life of your lease:

Capitalized cost. This is the price of the car. Think of it as the dealer's asking price. You want this number to be as low as possible, since the dealer will calculate your lease payments from here. (Hint: Never accept a capitalized cost that's as high as the car's regular sticker price.) Ideally you should check the car's invoice price and start haggling this number from there. The lower your capitalized cost, the lower your lease.

Residual value. This is a car's dollar value at the end of the lease, and it is always expressed as a percentage. You can double-check your dealer's math by getting a publication called *Automotive Lease Guide* ($12.50, available from Chart Software at 815-265-7831).

Money factor. This is the interest rate used to calculate your payments—a figure dealers don't give up too easily. When they do, it will be expressed as a decimal, like .0025. Simply multiply the figure by 24 to get the true annual percentage rate (APR), which is 6% in the present example. Conversely, you can figure the money factor from an interest rate by expressing the APR as a decimal (.06 in this example), then dividing by 24, for a money factor of .0025.

Once you are equipped with this data, your goal is to figure your *total lease cost.* In simplified fashion this amounts to the difference between the car's *capitalized cost* and its *residual value plus interest.*

To make sure you aren't paying a bloated amount, run the following calculation as supplied by James Bragg at *Fighting Chance*: this worksheet assumes a $20,000 car with a residual value of $10,000 leased for two years with an APR of 7.5%.

Divide depreciation by the lease term. In this example, $10,000/24 months = $416.66 per month. *This is what you pay monthly for depreciation.*

Add the capitalized cost to the residual value. ($20,000 + $10,000 = $30,000)

Multiply the result by the money factor. ($30,000 × .075/24 = $93.75.) *This is the monthly interest you pay.*

Add your depreciation ($416.66) plus interest ($93.75) for your *total monthly lease cost,* or $510.41 in this case, excluding taxes. If your numbers don't jibe with your dealer's contract, he's likely padded the numbers somewhere. Demand an explanation, or shop elsewhere.

Of course, not everybody has the head for such calculations. One excellent and easy tutorial is *Expert Lease* ($130 for Windows; 800-418-8450). The program comes with most of the numbers you'll need to perform a "lease-buy" analysis, plus invoice and retail prices for most recent model autos.

Five Money-Saving Lease Tips

PAN FOR GOLD WITH A FACTORY-SUBSIDIZED LEASE

Not all leases are lemons, mind you. In fact, some are knock-out deals. Chief among them are *factory-subsidized leases.* Underwritten by auto manufacturers, a factory-subsidized lease combines a below market interest rate with a high residual value—precisely the recipe for a fine lease bargain. Why would an automaker go out of its way to make a lease deal attractive? Because drivers who lease are more likely to be repeat customers than drivers who buy. These contracts, often available from Japanese makers, are easy to spot. Boldly advertised in large block type, they blare suspiciously low monthly payments. To make sure the promotion you see is a subsidized deal, ask your dealer for the car's residual value. If it is at least five percentage points higher than the value recorded in the *Automotive Lease Guide* (see page 36), you know you're driving a terrific lease deal. Japanese makers are especially known for offering generously subsidized leases.

AVOID UP-FRONT COSTS

You'll want to avoid siphoning your bank account just to get a lease rolling. Many contracts are quite top-heavy, however, requiring thousand-dollar-plus down payments and numerous other fees. Try to negotiate the down payment. Ask your dealer to either eliminate it altogether or reduce it by half.

LEASE EARLIER IN THE MODEL YEAR, NOT LATER

When purchasing a car outright, it is smartest to do your bargaining at the end of the model year, when dealers wish to clear their lots. In the game of leasing, however, the opposite rule applies. The logic here: by leasing earlier in the model year, you avoid any midyear price increases—sticker hikes that are sure to spike higher overall costs, including monthly payments. Prime leasing months are October through December, when it is possible to pluck next year's model fresh off the lot.

BREAKING A LEASE = BIG $ PENALTIES

You can choose lease terms of between two and five years. When mulling your options, remember that this is not a time to be fickle. Backing out of a lease will give you the worst sort of whiplash, subjecting you perhaps to all remaining payments on the lease. That's worth repeating. You may owe all remaining payments, car or no car. Still unsure about how long you should lease? One useful barometer is the manufacturer's bumper-to-bumper warranty. Since these generally last two to three years, a lease of similar duration protects you from paying any major repair bills yourself.

SHOP AROUND AS YOU WOULD FOR A NEW CAR

Compare notes on leases at several dealerships, *and haggle.* Just as in a straight car sale, you'll want to be certain you've covered your competitive bases.

PINCHING TIP
Don't be fooled by too-good-to-be-true lease ads. What appears as a "no money down" offer, for $100 per month, may end up being no more than a teaser designed to lure you to a showroom—where more costly options lurk. Be sure to read the fine print.

Buying a Used Car

Just a few years ago car buyers equated "used" with "abused." Buying an old automobile meant settling for someone else's transmission maladies—and demerits to your car-status quotient. No longer. Car experts agree that today's automakers are churning out better-quality products—cars that stand to perform, and look, as well in four years as they did when first driven off the lot.

To boot, drivers get more for their money in a secondhand set of wheels. A new car, for instance, loses about half of its value in the first two years of ownership. In subsequent years (for example, when it's considered "used") depreciation subsides and the car better holds its value. So go the used route and you will get more of what you pay for. Another perk: Insurance on some used models can be as much as 10% lower than on factory-fresh cars.

If you're still sour on the idea, consider the heavy supply of used cars today. On the heels of record leasing years—especially for luxury vehicles—the used-car market is saturated, with 30% more cars available these days than just three years ago. This Economics 101 lesson practically assures you a more-than-fair used-car price. On the trail of a used auto, you'll want to consider these tips:

SEEK OUT A USED MODEL WITH THE WARRANTY STILL IN EFFECT

Newer cars, especially luxury models, come with three-year, 36,000-mile warranties. Shop for a used car, if you can, with the warranty still in place. These handy warranties are often fully transferable to second owners and can save hundreds or even thousands in repair costs.

CHECK OUT "PRECERTIFIED" DEALS

With roughly 3 million cars coming off lease agreements annually, dealers are looking for ways to package these used mounts attractively. One new development: Makers like Lexus, Mercedes-Benz, and even Toyota are touting so-called precertified vehicles. For roughly $500 to $1,000 more than you'd pay otherwise, the precertified stamp assures that your car has passed a mechanic's checklist of 150 to 200 items. Better than vouching for the car's general health, precertification, in most cases, also gets you a full manufacturer's warranty.

KNOW YOUR PRICES

A dealer, of course, wants to make a respectable profit from any used car idling on the lot. You, on the other hand, want a fair price. What's that? The answer is only as far away as your local library, insurance office, or bank. Ask for the latest *Kelley Blue Book* or the *National Automobile Dealers Association Official Used Car Guide*. Each will offer regional information on most used-car models—specifically, both the average dealer purchase price and the selling price.

GUN FOR 15% BELOW A DEALER'S TAG

Flaunt your car smarts by tossing around a few of the figures you've picked up in the publications mentioned earlier. After your presentation, make him an offer of 15% below the asking price. (In most cases this still amounts to a dealer profit of a few hundred dollars.) If that fails, increase your bid by a tad, but by no more than 90% of the dealer's asking price. You know the rest—move on to the next dealer if the answer is no.

DO YOUR OWN INSPECTION TO AVOID LEMONS

Take this piece of advice no matter who's doing the selling. Hire an independent mechanic to give any car under consideration a clean bill of health. Compulsory tests should include a "body integrity check," which assesses damage from collisions, as well as compression tests for all cylinders. He'll also be on the lookout for any visible corrosion and suspicious noises emanating from the engine or transmission. If your candidate flunks any parts of the tests, use the low marks to negotiate the price down.

Smart Car Repair Strategies

It's no news flash to car owners that auto repair shops routinely land in the top three or four complaint categories at the nation's Better Business Bureaus. Repairing your car, however, doesn't have to be a nightmare. Assuming your vehicle is still under warranty, take it to a manufacturer-authorized dealer. Once it's driven past its warranty prime, you've got some investigating to do. Ask your friends—especially those who drive the same make car as you do—for recommendations. A good auto mechanic is as cherished as a good hairdresser or barber.

Seven strategies to keep your car in fine form without burning rubber in your wallet:

FIND OUT IF YOUR CAR HAS A "SECRET WARRANTY"

Each year, carmakers offer out-of-warranty repairs on certain models with mechanical or body defects. In most cases they fix the kinks for free, then send you on your way with a finely tuned car. Not all manufacturers are so generous. Sometimes they may not publicize a problem at all.

Got a fussy fuel pump? A peeling paint job? There may well be a silent recall in effect on your car. Mind you, the manufacturer is fully aware of the problem but simply fails to issue a public notice alerting car owners. Such maladies may be epidemic within a certain class of car and are problems that the manufacturer is willing to fix for free—for those who know to ask. Hence the term "secret warranty." Is your car under such a secret warranty? To find out, send information on your car's make and model year in a SASE to: Center for Auto Safety, 2001 "S" Street NW, Washington, D.C., 20009.

SEEK MULTIPLE ESTIMATES

Just as you would when shopping around for the best deal on anything, you'll want several mechanics to give you price quotes for the work to be done. Underline this rule twice if you drive a luxury car—a tip-off to mechanics that you've got money to burn.

SAVE BY SHUNNING THE DEALERSHIPS FOR MINOR REPAIRS

Once your warranty has expired, you'll have the not too happy task of finding a mechanic you can trust. Sure, you can simply return to the dealership. But surveys have shown that service departments at dealerships are slow and costly. Save anywhere from 20% to 50% by using an independent mechanic for simple jobs like installing new brakes or mufflers.

LOOK FOR CREDENTIALS

There's no Mechanic's U, but the field does offer some certifications. Make sure any mechanic has passed muster with the National Institute for Automotive Service Excellence. The sharpest shops also send their mechanics to several training classes per year. So ask.

TALK TO THE MECHANIC YOURSELF FOR BETTER SERVICE

Not everybody talks to the mechanic who works on their car. For better service, you should. Those mechanics who do a lot of the talking themselves—asking you questions about your car— are more reliable than the silent types.

GET YOUR REPAIRS SPELLED OUT IN WRITING

This is the only way to ensure that extra fiddling, at considerable cost, won't happen at your expense. Ask for a written estimate and a copy of the mechanic's order form, and insist that it require your verbal or written okay for any additional work.

GET COMFY UNDER A HOOD YOURSELF

Perhaps the best way to foil repair scams is to know a bit about your car's inner workings. Most community colleges offer inexpensive auto repair classes. Taking one will let you talk shop, literally, with mechanics and reduce your chances of being taken for a ride.

CYBERTIP

Drivers with access to the Web should race to Financenter (http://www.financenter.com), a personal finance resource center with page after page of information for car and home shoppers. Packed with individual "calculators," the site lets you figure car payments, size up lease deals, and much more.

SAVE WITH SISTER ACTS

Try parking a Geo Prism next to a Toyota Corolla. Think you're seeing double? Indeed you are. These cars, like other auto "twins," are manufactured in the very same plant, have the same body structure, engines, and transmissions. There's one difference: price. The Prism runs about $1,500 less than the Corolla—a real bargain for what experts consider a better car. Unlike its competitor, the Prism has quick antilock brakes, and its warranty includes 24-hour roadside assistance, far more generous than the Corolla's.

Other car siblings worth checking out: the Buick Century, Oldsmobile Cutlass, and Chevy Malibu. All have the same structure, engine, and transmission, just slightly different styling. The Malibu is the best deal, at about $16,000; the other two run $2,000–$4,000 more. Similarly, the Acura SLX ($34,320) is the spitting image of the Isuzu Trooper ($25,805). The difference in these models is in the options: the Acura comes fully loaded.

CHAPTER 3

First-Class Savings for Travelers

So you want to take off *Casablanca* style, with, say, six steamer trunks and a butler in tow. But your wallet doth protest: You've got a mortgage to pay. A 401(k) to feed. A finicky muffler to replace. Is there any hope, then, for your travel-mag fantasies to spring to life? Yes, you can travel above your means and still come in under budget.

Did you know:

- Each year the airlines offer discounts and promotions worth billions of dollars, but fliers take advantage of just 1% of them?
- The nation's 3.5 million hotel rooms, on average, are filled to just 65% of capacity nightly, giving travelers lots of negotiating leverage?
- An upgraded airline seat or hotel room may be yours simply for the asking?

Understanding What a
Travel Agent Can Do for You

Even though their skills are fast being challenged by on-line reservations programs and other do-it-yourself offerings, travel agents still deserve your notice. If you know how to use them wisely, they can add significant value to your trip—or slice its cost.

But first, some background. Because they work on commissions from the airlines and other travel suppliers, agents' impartiality has long come into question. If agents rely on bonuses and other perks from the trade, goes the argument, how can they serve their clients' needs without bias?

Indeed, in recent years, studies—including one conducted by **MONEY** magazine—have found some agents lacking in their ability to pinpoint the lowest airfares and package deals. Even so, the consumer's best advocate on the travel agent front is economics: in order to stay afloat in increasingly competitive times, travel agents *must* provide good, fair service to lure you back.

To find the absolute best agent for you, start by *making sure yours is reputable.* Personal referrals are usually the best way to go. Barring that, one credential you might look for is the certified travel counselor (CTC) designation. Since agents aren't certified in most states, the CTC at least guarantees that an agent has five years' experience and has taken an intensive series of travel-planning courses.

Next, *know what you want.* If you merely need airline tickets, any number of agents can fill your needs. For help with more complex itinerary planning, you may need a different type of pro. Many agencies, for instance, have begun to specialize in one or two areas, such as cruises, adventure travel, and family-oriented packages. So be sure to quiz an agent on his or her expertise.

Finally, *take a test flight—sort of.* Just as you would interview, say, an accountant or broker, it makes good sense to sit down with a prospective travel agent to get a feel for their business practices. How much time will they spend arranging your trip? Can they grant you any special perks? Do they have a 24-hour emergency number available to customers? Above all, do they seem accommodating to your needs without being pushy?

Regardless of the agent or agency you choose, here is a brief tour of the money-saving moves a cherished travel pro can make for you.

• **'Round-the-clock fare searches.** It pays to ask an agent about their technoskills. Thanks to a spate of jazzy airline reservations technology, some agents can search compulsively for the lowest airfare while they sleep—literally. A number of computer programs will scan fares around the clock to make sure yours is the best deal. If it finds a better price, it will rebook you at the lowest fare.

• **Access to discount hotel rates.** Getting a bargain hotel rate remains one of travel's great conundrums (more on this science later). Because most belong to hotel consortiums—low-rate clearinghouses, so to speak—travel agents can sometimes quote you prices of 15%–30% below retail. An agent's booking may also give you "run of house" privileges, meaning you'll be entitled to the best room available at no extra charge.

• **A way to buy fliers more time.** Most airlines demand full payment of your nonrefundable airline ticket within 24 hours of making a reservation. With approximately 100,000 fare changes each day, passengers may feel queasy about committing to a price so hastily. A travel agent who values your business can buy you more time by holding some reservations for as long as 72 hours. Those extra days allow you to tweak your travel plans further and perhaps find a cheaper deal. Even better, because of their clout with the airlines, agents can sometimes get you a preferred two- or three-week advance fare with just one week's notice.

• **Free airline upgrades.** While no agent can routinely shower you with free upgrades, some can toss one your way from time to time. That's because airlines often give agencies upgrade certificates to keep business aloft; in turn, many give them away as marketing tools. The beneficiaries? Good, reliable customers like you.

• **Last-minute vacation bulletins.** Tour operators snap up vacation packages in bulk—way before they have any takers. When they fail to attract enough passengers to fill their inventory, they've got to unload them fast. After all, an airline seat and a hotel room are fast depreciating commodities. A good agent can be your ticket to last-minute price slashes, saving you as much as 20–30%.

Keep in mind, you stand to get the most perks and the best service from an agency that cherishes your business. So don't start demanding special favors if you've booked only once or twice with an agency. Let them know, however, that you are an excellent prospective longtime client. As with any spending venue, customer loyalty can pay off exponentially in the long term.

Flying on the Cheap

The nation's 498 million airline passengers spend about 30% of their travel budget on plane tickets. *Ignoranti!* (stupid). *Bête!* (stupid). You get the idea. We'd much rather you use that money to, say, eat more Brie.

But what is the "best fare"? Much like solving Rubik's Cube, plucking the magic low number from an arcane system of 100,000 daily price fluctuations often boils down to plain old luck. While "advance purchase tickets," typically 14- and 21-day advance fares, are hypothetically the best deals, this is not always the case. It is entirely possible to net a better fare the day before a departure than by booking two or three weeks out.

The surest way to get a great fare is to *be flexible*. Often, shifting your departure date by just a day or two can make a big dent in your fare. So have an agent check for multiple departure times that are convenient. And don't forget any alternate airports that you might use—such as Oakland Airport for San Francisco and Orange County Airport for Los Angeles International. Fares to these secondary strips can be as much as 40% less than flying into the major city terminal.

Here are other ways to lower your air travel costs.

• **Keep an eye on fares after you book.** Don't tear your newspaper to shreds when you find an ad hawking a lower price than you've paid. Just fight back. If you've bought a refundable ticket and the fare difference is big enough—say, more than $75—you can get at least some of that money back. Have your travel agent, or the airline, reissue you a new ticket at the lower rate. Of course, you will have to fork over a reissue fee, typically about $50. But for a ticket that drops from $600 to $350—not an unlikely scenario—it sure pays.

• **Slug your way through fare wars.** In any given calendar year, count on the airlines to announce between six and eight major sales—fare wars, in travel parlance.

Negotiating the price battle is tricky. The airlines allot less than 10% of their seats to these sales, and they go faster than the Concorde. And just as one airline is busy clipping its fares, competing carriers are busy in a game of one-upsmanship—perhaps driving prices even lower.

Some travel experts will tell you to sit on the sidelines when a sale begins, on the chance that fares will continue to slide. Don't risk it. Sure, hedging your bets is good form in poker, but when the airlines are talking Paris for $248 roundtrip, pack your beret. You know a rare fare when you see one.

Three ways to play the wars:

Plan ahead. This isn't *Mission Impossible.* Let your travel agent know the routes you're likely to fly—Des Moines to visit your aunt, for instance. Equipped with personal travel preferences, they can spring on any great fares for you. Also try to block your vacation time in advance, giving you the freedom to act on any fare wars that erupt beforehand.

Book a reservation, but wait 24 hours to pay while you continue to shop around. Once that grace period ends, however, go with your original plan or you may forfeit your reservation. Waiting a few days in the hopes that fares will drop another $50 is simply not a good gamble.

Call every carrier that serves the route you want to fly. Chances are they have lowered their fares, too—or will soon.

• **For last-minute treks, try consolidators.** Those matchbox-size ads in your Sunday travel section can be jewel boxes indeed. Trumpeting low fares to exotic places like Bombay (and, more recently, domestic cities like Los Angeles), they've probably made you squint at least a time or two. But who's behind these deals, and are they really legitimate?

The airlines don't want you to know this, but they routinely dump seats in the laps of travel wholesalers called "consolidators," at vastly reduced prices. Why? Because they know they can't sell every seat, and they are willing to let the discount market pick up the slack. The result is a slew of cheap airline seats going for 30% to 50% off published prices. Last-minute travelers, in particular, stand to profit from consolidators because most shops don't adhere to "advance purchase rules." Today, both foreign and domestic tickets are available at consolidators large and small, as well as at some travel agencies. Most are on regularly scheduled airlines and are nonrefundable, so you must be sure about your travel dates.

A few hitches: Consolidator tickets are generally exempt from a carrier's frequent flier programs, and some direct-sounding routes (say, New York to London) may involve a layover. So ask before you book. And some smaller consolidators take only cash—a setup to avoid since paying by credit card gives you recourse if the booking goes awry. To locate a consolidator who services the routes you want, contact World Travel Network (800-409-6753), a nationwide consolidator clearinghouse.

• **Go courier.** New York to Hong Kong for $350, roundtrip. Los Angeles to Bangkok for $100. Sound too good to be true? Not for free-lance air couriers, who save up to 85% off standard ticket prices. You've probably read or heard about these gigs: in exchange for carrying a freight company's shipping documents, travelers get laughably cheap fares. To many folks the idea seems a bit shady, as if contraband is somehow part of the deal. Not so.

But just to allay any fears of impropriety, here's a rundown of how it works. Freight companies have shipments to move (usually of paper documents such as canceled checks) in a speedy fashion. Commercial freight is costly and takes days to clear customs. By purchasing baggage space on a regular passenger flight, however, these companies haul their stuff to its destination much more quickly and cheaply. To do it, though, they need a ticket-holding passenger (that's where you come in), enabling them to buy up any excess baggage space on your flight. Your only duty is to carry the shipping documents and pass them along to the courier representative at flight's end.

More than 60 courier companies nationwide service routes in Asia, South America, Europe, even the Caribbean. Booking is fairly simple, as long as you understand the rules. In most cases, only carry-on luggage is permitted, and a trip's duration may vary from three to 30 days or longer. The later you wait to book, the cheaper your flight is likely to be (in some cases it may even be free). The downside: Traveling with a companion can be tough to arrange, unless he or she is willing to pay for a full-fare ticket. Some companies will work with couples, however, to accommodate consecutive day trips or even same-day departures.

For a more thorough glimpse into the courier world, write for a free copy of *The Shoestring Traveler.* This is the official publication of the International Association of Air Couriers, which for a $45 annual membership fee will alert you to daily last-minute specials offered by dozens of companies worldwide. Contact them at P.O. Box 1349, Lake Worth, Fla. 33460; or call 407-582-8320 (or you can find them on the Web at http://www.courier.org).

- **Use a niche or regional airline—but book in advance.** You may have noticed, however, that fares on carriers like Southwest, Vanguard, Midway, and others aren't always el cheapo anymore. In fact, their regular fares to cities such as San Antonio and Oakland, California, can be just as much as on the big airlines.

You get the best deals from these guys by buying way in advance. Take that Los Angeles–to–Oakland fare. By booking two weeks in advance, you could've traveled in 1996 for about $25 one way on Southwest Airlines, lower than any other carrier. Waiting until the last minute, however, can put your fare right back up there with the major airlines. So buy as far in advance as possible, and call to compare prices.

- **Seek age-specific discounts.** Got gray hair? Long hair? Smart senior citizens and students alike stand to profit from discounts ranging from 15% to 30%. Most airlines give a 10% break on fares for folks over 62. Some sweeten the deal if you fly more often. For example, seniors can also buy coupon booklets (available with most carriers) entitling them to fly between four and six one-way segments, for about $600.

Other big savers are reserved for students aged 14 to 24. Airlines like TWA offer five-in-a-book domestic coupons, similar to elder discounts, for about $550, valid for a year. Delta has also touted fares of $138 to $318 round-trip, good for a student *and two additional passengers.* In addition, American Express has been known to offer its young cardholders two discount coupons per year, for $159 to $299 round-trip within the continental United States.

• **"Split" your airfare, and other flying tricks.** You may have read, in some publications, about an airline ticket ploy to beat the high tariff often paid when flying into a major hub city such as Dallas or Chicago. Called "hidden city fares," the technique involves booking a ticket to your flight's *ultimate* destination (say, San Antonio via Dallas) and getting off the plane at the first stop. Curiously, fares to a plane's final destination are often lower than those to the hub you want. Voilà! By scooting off the plane, you've saved perhaps hundreds of dollars. But because the airlines insist this practice is technically against their rules, we won't delve any further here (wink). So research among yourselves (and don't check any baggage).

Moving on to a perfectly aboveboard tactic can save you 70% on certain routes, especially if traveling last minute, when fares crest. Called "splitting fares," a term coined by Tom Parsons at *Best Fares* magazine, this method requires only that you buy two tickets: one to an intermediate city, such as Albuquerque; then a second to your final destination, Dallas, in this scenario. Your one-way fare (recently $204 in this case) can be cheaper than one direct or nonstop fare ($514). A good travel agent can help you do this, or any one of several on-line services can give you the information you need to construct your best route (see pages 56–57).

• **Manage your frequent flier programs like an invest-ment portfolio.** Frequent traveler reward programs come in so many guises these days, managing them is like figuring out some complex family tree. Even so, you really can't go wrong signing on for the bonanzas offered by airlines and hotel chains: they're free. But that's only the beginning. Getting your share of free miles depends on how well you play the awards game.

The most profitable plan? *Remain loyal to as few suppliers as possible.* If you fly numerous times a year, for instance, make it your business to rack up as many miles as possible with one or two carriers (of course, this assumes that fares on other airlines are competitive).

Tip number two: *Redeem airline miles only when you need to.* Remember how many backaches it took you to earn them? Typically a domestic ticket costs 25,000. To wring every ounce of value from that freebie, then, use it on a route that rarely goes on sale.

Get even more steam from that airline freebie by taking the free side trip you're entitled to. Many people don't realize it, but most airlines allow you to make one week-long stopover on free tickets. For example, if you are traveling between New York and Honolulu, the airline will permit you to sight-see in an intermediate city, such as Los Angeles. Even paying passengers don't get this sort of perk, unless they are traveling on a full coach fare.

• **Go on-line for deals.** These days passengers have access to several electronic tools once exclusive to travel agents. While many hotel chains and car rental companies have their own Websites, to date the most sophisticated and cost-conscious services are airline or airfare oriented.

Users of on-line programs such as CompuServe, Prodigy, and America Online can tap into numerous travel sources that let you do your own shopping and price comparisons. Most allow you to book reservations. And since they are updated hundreds of times each day, these programs may even give you a jump on fare wars by alerting you to sale prices before ads hit the newspapers.

One such option, easySABRE (available on all three major on-line services), lets you plow through thousands of fares and itineraries to land the best prices. A new feature on the service, called Flightfinder, will even canvas over 900 itinerary possibilities and pop up the three cheapest.

CYBERTIP

Want a fast, free alert to airline fare wars, as they erupt? By subscribing to the Traveler's Net "Fare War Mailing List," you'll get e-mail notification of fare wars on the same day airlines announce them. This gives you a better chance to grab those limited seats. Simply sign up for the service on-line (http://www.travelersnet.com).

CYBERTIP

Several airlines are gearing up their own Websites that let you preview deals and participate in free-for-all "seat auctions." You may even find some fares that are advertised only on their Websites. One of the best to check out: American Airlines (http://www.americanair.com), which posts lots of discounted flights that travel through its Dallas hub. Another, Cathay Pacific (http://www.cathay-usa.com), holds regular auctions for seats to Asia.

Pay the Absolute Lowest Hotel Rates

Getting the lowest price on any of the nation's 3.5 million hotel rooms is akin to searching for the Ark. Some pros advise calling hotels directly to get the magic rate; others insist that hotel chains' 800 numbers are the way to go. Diehards want you to go one further, by walking in and demanding the best price of the night. Sort of like negotiating for soon-to-be day-old bread. Truth is, *all three strategies are excellent, and you should try them all.* Call the 800 number first, then the hotel directly to see if they can beat the rate you're quoted. (A tip: Call during the day in order to get the most knowledgeable hotel staff on the phone.) Finally, upon check-in, do a little sleuthing. Before giving your name, inquire about the lowest rates of the day. If they quote you a better room price than what you've booked, they'll have to honor it.

Bottom line: No one need ever pay published hotel rates, or "rack rates," as they call them in the business. Why? Because as we mentioned earlier, hotels rarely fill up. Here are more strategies:

• **Check out corporate rates.** Always worth a shot, the proverbial "corporate rate" is available to many travelers. The catch: Such rates are harder to come by these days. In the past, anyone could phone up Hotel Central and demand a corporate rate, for a typical savings of about 10%–20%. No longer. Having wised up, hotels now are much more likely to ask for your corporate affiliation. And unless your employer has a corporate account with the place, you're out of luck. So read on. . . .

• **Book through a hotel consolidator.** Much like airline consolidators previously discussed, these outfits buy up blocks of rooms, then resell them to the public, passing along their volume discount. In the process, you stand to save anywhere from 20% to 50% off rack rates. Even when hotels are technically filled to capacity, some consolidators can still get you in, since they have committed to buy blocs of rooms way in advance.

Hotel Reservations Network (800-964-6835) is the largest hotel consolidator, with all types of hotel rooms available in New York, San Francisco, Chicago, Boston, Orlando, Miami, and San Diego.

Express Reservations (800-356-1123) offers a wide selection of budget, chain, and luxury hotel selections in New York and Los Angeles, from $89 to $250.

Central Reservations Service (800-950-0232) handles mid-priced hotel rooms in New York, San Francisco, Miami, and Orlando. Rates run from $55 for a budget room in Miami to $200 for suite accommodations in New York.

• **Use your employee discounts.** Don't forget—many large corporations negotiate preferred rates with a wide variety of properties. Lower than both published rack and corporate rates, these prices, generally 30% below rack, are usually available to employees for personal use. Use them.

• **Tap into other preferred rates.** If you don't have the benefit of special rates through your job, here's a good remedy. Travelgraphics International publishes a guide that will check you into over 10,000 hotels and resorts worldwide, cheaply. Each property is listed with a code, which nets you savings of 10% to 60%. Formerly available only to travel agents, the *Worldwide Hotel Rate Directory* is now sold to the public (the 1996 edition costs $22, including shipping and handling). To get a copy, call 800-644-8785.

• **Guarantee overseas reservations in U.S. dollars**. Going overseas, travelers are subject to currency fluctuations that can swell a bill by 10% or more. You can avoid this scenario by guaranteeing your overseas hotel room in U.S. currency. When making a reservation or dealing with a travel agent, make sure you get a dollar quote that is good for the duration of your stay. These rates are available through most large chain hotels.

Buying a Package Vacation

Maybe a prefab vacation—one that includes air, hotel, and a few other extras—is too generic for your taste. Think twice. These days package vacations come highly customized, with your choice of accommodations (condos to suites), meal plans, and rental car options. Even better, a package deal can yield substantial savings, especially to destinations that have costly components, like Disney World (daily park fees), the Caribbean (island tours and transfers), and ski villages such as Aspen and Vail (lift tickets, equipment rental).

Fortunately you need not perform any complex algorithms to get a great bundled deal. The major airlines offer very competitive package pricing, and some independent tour operators, advertising through your Sunday newspaper, let you book directly. If you do book through a travel agent, ask for extras, such as dining coupons and airport transfers. You'll do even better if you heed these tips.

• **Know what you're getting.** Typically, a package vacation bundles airfare, hotel accommodations, car rental, and/or round-trip airport transfers in the price. Airlines and tour operators can assemble such trips together much more cheaply than you, using volume discounts and the like. Even so, you should ask your travel provider to break down the elements of the package for you, comparing them against what you might pay for each item separately. (If you feel you are being steered to one package over another for no apparent reason, don't hesitate to ask your agent how much of a bonus he or she stands to make from your trip.)

• **Travel off season and save up to 50%.** We aren't hyping travel to Vail when the slopes have gone bald. And we don't wish you in Bali during the monsoon season. But a little flexibility in your itinerary can add up to big bucks. Hotels and resorts tend to fill up during high, or peak, seasons—January and February for ski resorts, ditto for the Caribbean. So expect no bargains then. The same places may beg for visitors, however, during their low season (when they have the least traffic) or in shoulder season (falling between high and low periods).

How does that affect your wallet? Depending on where you

care to play, packing your bags during a destination's *low and shoulder seasons* will save you 15%–50% right off the bat. Even adjusting your itinerary by just one day, as the following table shows, can shave hundreds from your bill.

So avoid the crowds. Check with your travel agent to find out dates for low and shoulder seasons for your destination of choice. A sampling of savings:

DESTINATION	HIGH SEASON RATE	LOW/SHOULDER SEASON RATE	SAVINGS
Fla. golf and tennis resort (daily room rates)	$200 (Oct. 1–Dec. 21)	$130 (May 1–Sept. 30)	35%
Nassau all-inclusive, (7 nights, pp)	$1,017 (Jan. 6–Feb. 9)	$784 (Feb. 10–March 30)	23%
Williamsburg, Va., deluxe resort (daily room rates)	$325 (April, May, Oct.)	$265 (Jan. and Feb.)	18%
Tucson, Ariz., golf resort (daily room rates)	$240 (Jan. 10–May 24)	$125 (May 25–June 30)	48%

• **Use a cruise-only agency to set sail.** Travel agencies are segmenting, or specializing, like mad. One such niche is cruising, with more than 800 so-called cruise-only shops now booking berths for U.S. passengers. The advantage is clear. You get the undivided expertise of a cruise pro, someone who's really got sea legs and knows about ships. On top of that, you're getting a discount of 20% to 60% below published fares. This is a great boon, since in the cruise business discounts are available from the cruise lines directly only if you book nine months to a year in advance. Dealing with a cruise-only agency gives you more leeway.

An example of savings comes from the Ft. Lauderdale–based World Wide Cruises (800-882-9000), which offers price breaks of 20%–55% on all major cruise lines, plus cabin upgrades where available. For high-end, nondiscounting ships, the agency gives shipboard credits worth about $500.

For a list of cruise-only agencies in your area, contact National Association of Cruise Only Agencies, 3191 Coral Way, Suite 630, Miami, Fla. 33145.

• **Try a travel club.** For those who sock away savings for a special vacation each year, a travel club makes good sense. The most popular, and promising, variety are *discount services* that entitle members to a wide range of discounts at hotels and restaurants. They work this way: For a fee of anywhere from $20 to $100, club members get an ID card and a fat book listing participating hotels, restaurants, and other travel concerns such as attractions and car rental companies. Claiming your discount is as simple as calling the reservations numbers provided and/or whipping out your card upon arrival. Savings are generous—as much as half off published rates at many establishments. The service you choose, however, should depend on where and how you travel. The largest such clubs include the following:

Entertainment Travel Editions (800-445-4137) publishes 120 city-specific guidebooks ($30–$50) good in the United States, Canada, the Caribbean, and Europe. Most coupons allow for hotel discounts of up to 50% off rack rates, as well as two-for-one dining at dozens of restaurants. Also, their *National Hotel Directory* ($27.95) gets you as much as 50% off at over 3,500 hotels and resorts, plus discounts at local attractions.

Quest International (800-325-2400) puts out a directory of savings of 50% on over 2,100 hotels in the United States,

Caribbean, Mexico, Canada, and Europe. It also includes hotel dining discounts of 25%, plus $100 off cruises on Carnival cruise lines. Membership fee: $99.

International Travel Card 50 (800-342-0558) touts rates of half off more than 3,800 hotels (mainly budget to midprice hotels); also comes with a dining directory good at 1,000 restaurants (mostly two-for-one discounts). Fee: $36.

• **Consider going "all-inclusive."** It was the cruise industry, back in the 1970s, that christened the "all-inclusive" vacation. Step on board, and almost everything was covered, from buffet blowouts to nightly cabarets, even round-trip airfare to and from your port of departure. Today the all-inclusive concept has taken off dramatically and notably on Caribbean islands, where most properties (six out of 10) at least offer the all-inclusive option.

Before booking, shop around and ask your travel agent to *break out all elements of the trip* as you would with any other package. Are those extras—like free drinks and water sports— worth the additional dough? Or would you pay the same rate for a vacation with fewer amenities? It's crucial to know what you're getting, since every travel provider has a different definition of "all-inclusive." To some, the moniker fits if airfare, hotel, and meals are included. Others go a lot further, including unlimited alcohol, sight-seeing excursions, airport transfers, and taxes in the price. Make sure that all the features you desire (such as sports, airport transfers, and perhaps drinks) are included in the price—otherwise you may be better off going à la carte.

PINCHING TIP

Booking a package vacation? Make sure that the price includes all hotel and city taxes, which can add as much as 23% to your bill. Otherwise that $150 nightly rate on Fantasy Island may cost you $184 per night.

Save More—and Get More—During Your Trip

If you've planned wisely, you will have realized your greatest savings before setting foot on a plane. Remember, those who ask (for things like upgrades and other amenities) do receive. Only shy types need settle for standard rooms and run-of-the mill service. Don't be one of them.

• **Charm your way into first or business class.** Never demand. Just ask, in your most charming voice, "Any chance of getting an upgrade today?" Look blasé, as if that big leather seat doesn't mean the world to you. You've got nothing to lose, and only more legroom and free drinks to gain. Count on a success rate of roughly one free upgrade for every 15 or 20 tries—well worth your gumption. For those traveling the same route regularly, it pays to learn the gate agents' names. Chocolates and flowers do wonders, too.

• **Ask for a better price, and a better room, at check-in.** Even if you have a rock-bottom price. Desk clerks and managers have more power than you think and may drop the price because they like your suit. Just be polite and never demanding. Casually ask if the hotel is booked to capacity, if there is an executive or suite level, and could you possibly get one of those rooms for the price you're quoted. If you are a frequent guest, remind them of this. Members of frequent stay programs such as Hilton's Honors are automatically entitled to a room upgrade, when available, upon booking a corporate rate.

• **Get the best exchange rates in foreign countries.** When visiting foreign countries, you'll want to stretch your U.S. dollars to the max. To get the best possible exchange rates for lire, yen, or francs, remember a few things:

Credit cards, believe it or not, cut you the best deals when paying for hotels, meals, or shopping sprees. That's because most issuers will extend *wholesale exchange rates* to card users—rates far more generous than what you'd get on your own. Expect to pay a commission, of course, of roughly 1% on each foreign purchase. But you'll still come out ahead, getting about 5% more for your dollar.

For cash purchases, forget about traveler's checks, which tweak you coming (a 1% fee to buy them) and going (many places charge to redeem them, too). A better alternative these days is to simply carry your *bank ATM card.* Most systems will let you access your account just as you would at home. Foreign transaction fees may vary anywhere from $1 to $2, but the favorable exchange rate (again, typically a wholesale rate) and lack of commission still put you way ahead. A tip before you leave home: Check to see if your bank requires a four-digit pin number to access your account overseas. Some institutions have this minor hitch.

• **Pinch dollars when you dial home.** Pick up that hotel room phone at your peril. Standard surcharges for calls billed to your room run between $1 and $4, or up to 300% above the actual price of the call itself. And forget about dialing out late at night for lower rates. Most hotels charge premium rates around the clock, stuffing any savings into their own coffers. Worse, hotels rarely post the duration of phone calls on your bill, making errors hard to spot.

Avoid a phone sting by toting your own phone card and using your own long-distance carrier. Hotels may charge you 50 cents or so to access the carriers listed below, but that's still cheaper than the alternative. Access numbers for the three largest long-distance services are

AT&T: 800-3210-ATT
MCI: 800-950-1022
Sprint: 800-877-8000

Should you have trouble connecting to your carrier, it may be by design. Some hotels secretly block access to other carriers, forcing you to dial direct. Should this happen, complain to the hotel front desk and ask to have any access charges removed from your bill.

Of course, you can always head to the lobby pay phone for friendlier service. Alas, for the jet-lagged and bedbound who truly must dial direct, heed this tip: ring your party no more than four or five times. Otherwise the hotel may bill you for the first minute anyway.

• **Save on rented wheels.** When you're traveling in the United States, your best bet for a rental car deal rests in a *fly/drive deal*. Offered by the major airlines in conjunction with the big car rental agencies, these plans throw in a rental car for a negligible sum—sometimes less than $100 per week. When renting a car separately, *think small*. Though biggies like Avis and Hertz dominate the rental arena by far, their small competitors, such as Enterprise and Dollar, offer wheels for up to 50% less.

Once you're ready to sign a rental contract, remember two things. First, you may want to pass on the company's insurance (known as a *collision damage waiver*). This costly coverage runs anywhere from $10 to $15 per day. Your own auto insurance, or in some cases your credit card, protects you equally or better. Finally, don't go for the rental company's fuel option (they sell you a full tank of gas, up front, at competitive prices) unless you think you'll return the car with an empty tank.

CHAPTER 4

Don't Break the Bank

How to Save on Your Checking, Savings, and Credit Card Accounts (Plus Tips for Borrowers)

You might not think of your bank—with its forbidding vaults and uniformed guards—as the place to reenact Bob Barker's *Let's Make a Deal*. Yet as the banking industry piles on record profits exceeding $40 billion annually, consumers have every right to speak up and demand the most favorable terms they can get.

To minimize banking costs in today's climate of megamergers, consumers especially need to watch their step. Clever marketers, you see, would have you believe that one-stop banking— parking your checking, savings accounts, loans, and credit cards under one roof—conserves both time and money. Sure, the corner teller may be handy, but *your loyalty to Friendly BankCorp can actually cost you,* in the form of a competitor's fatter CD yields or an out-of-state lender's lower interest rates. Whether you're angling for a personal loan or grumbling over high checking account charges, you *can* get superior deals.

Mind Your Fees

What has your banker done for you lately? For the millions of depositors nationwide, the answer is probably "Raised fees." Fully 85% of all institutions impose them, up from just 35% in 1991. Some customers are being asked to pay $3 for teller services, while others get nicked by as much as $4 to use the humble ATM. Overall, fees have soared by 112% since 1985, giving the term "bank robber" a whole new meaning.

When shopping for a bank, then, or even if you're thinking of switching, you'll want to deploy *fee strategy number one: Know which fees apply to you and fight back.* Shop around carefully, taking note of each institution's battery of fees. How many will apply to you? Are they the lowest in your vicinity? By reducing or eliminating some of the charges mentioned above and below, a typical depositor might pay herself back about $100 per year. If you are a veteran customer—especially one who maintains high balances in a number of accounts—revolt! Head straight to your branch manager and ask for relief on some of the more outrageous fees. These may include returned check fees (as much as $25); photocopy fees for lost checks ($5 at some banks); hourly charges of up to $25 for basic account troubleshooting; and a galling 10% levy to exchange coins for bills.

Annoyingly, fees can even gnarl your basic checking habits. A reasonable depositor might hope for an account that combines low monthly fees and a respectable interest rate on their balances, right? Alas, such animals are rare at most banks, which brings us to *fee strategy number two: Find the right checking account fit.* Large banks offer as many as six different types of checking accounts. They go by many names, such as NOW accounts and day-to-day accounts. They may appear to be cut from the same cloth, but they are not: one might charge monthly maintenance fees while another springs you for keeping an average daily balance of $1,000 or more. The Cadillac account probably lets you write free unlimited checks, but the put-put variety charges a flat fee to make eight to 10 transactions per month.

Have you got the right one? Your individual banking style can help answer that question and save you a bundle in monthly fees. Start by carefully reviewing your monthly banking statements. How many checks, on average, do you write each month? What about ATM runs? Is your checking balance fairly consistent or erratic? After scouring your records, call or visit your bank's customer service department. Request descriptions of each of their checking options, and ask if a particular account type can save you cash. One example: Let's assume you're currently paying the standard $12 for an interest-bearing account but keep a low balance and have bare-bones checking and ATM activity. By switching to a basic account—$3 per month for eight ATM and checking transactions—you'd likely save at least $100 per year.

Earlier we hinted at how a fat bank balance (or combination of balances) can nix your checking charges. Now, before you go stuffing funds in the bank to qualify for that "free checking" prize, consider *fee strategy number three: Don't let fees drive your banking habits altogether.* For example, plenty of institutions tout "free" checking, plus nominal interest, as long as you keep a few grand hanging around in the account. Sounds nifty—unless, that is, you write only $500 worth of checks per month and get a paltry interest of 1.4% on your money. If this describes your banking MO, "free checking" may be a bum deal. Instead, keep only the amount you need in checking, paying modest fees on the account if you must. Put the rest of your cash to hard work elsewhere, such as in one of the higher-yielding vehicles discussed below.

PINCHING TIP

Safety saves. And whether you've got your bank deposits in checking accounts or CDs, it is insured by the Federal Deposit Insurance Corporation for up to $100,000. Hopefully your bank won't ever fail. To be supersafe, though, check the stability of your bank with Veribanc, the Wakefield, Massachusetts, firm specializing in bank and thrift evaluations. You can request a summary report on any U.S. financial institution for $10 by calling 800-837-4226.

Earn More Money on
Your Checking Deposits

Yes, we've just finished lecturing on the best bank checking account for your needs. After all, you probably pay most of your bills, and even trace back your monthly spending, with this popular account type. But guess what? You may be able to delete your bank's checking fees and other hassles with one of the these three alternatives.

If you have access to a credit union, don't overlook *credit union checking accounts.* Forget that candy bowl at your bank. Credit unions offer much sweeter deals on most types of accounts, including checking. Credit unions are nonprofit organizations, allowing them to outpace most bank rates. Specifically, credit union checking accounts *pay about 50% more than bank also-rans.* Often called *credit union share draft accounts,* these beauts work just like the account at your local bank, but with an edge. Offering more than lavish rates, they spoil you with lower monthly fees, too.

The one hurdle you must clear: access. Most credit unions are open to a specific universe of customers, such as state employees. With credit union membership growing by about two million folks annually, however, chances are better than ever that you can find one to take you in. For instance, if you have a relative who has ever joined the Pentagon Federal Credit Union (a military credit union with over 500,000 members), you can probably sign up, too. For more leads on credit unions you may be eligible to join, contact the Credit Union National Association (800-358-5701).

If you maintain a balance of at least $5,000, *a money market fund* is another route around stingy bank checking accounts. Not to be confused with a bank's money-market deposit accounts, these vehicles invest in safe instruments like Treasuries and pay roughly twice the going rate for bank checking accounts. In early 1996 that was as much as 5.6%. Some money funds even toss in free checks. (Now when was the last time your friendly bank offered a perk like that?)

Maybe the idea of writing checks on a money-market fund sounds a tad esoteric, a bit too hands-off. Fact is, handling basic checking needs with a money-market fund isn't at all inconvenient. Depositors who call a fund's 800 number receive both a prospectus and an application for the fund. After you send your check deposit, most will let you write unlimited checks (minimum amounts of $100 to $500 may apply). To find the best money-market fund rates available nationwide, check the pages of **MONEY** magazine each month, where such rates are listed in the "Money Monitor" section. You can obtain an even more complete listing of rates from a newsletter called *100 Highest Yields*. To subscribe to the weekly publication, contact Bank Rate Monitor (800-327-7717), the leading source for bank rates.

If you need a short-term holding place for your cash, and keep your check writing to a minimum, then consider a bank's *money-market deposit account*. As mentioned earlier, these are supersafe, federally insured accounts that can beat standard savings rates by nearly two percentage points. Rates fluctuate with short-term interest rates and can gyrate wildly over a span of just two or three months. You'll get the healthiest money-market deposit rates (surprise) by venturing out of state. The sources named on the previous page can help you troll for the best rates and terms.

Stock and bond owners can enjoy yet another high-yielding haven for checking funds: *asset-management accounts,* also known as *brokerage firm cash-management accounts.* A hybrid of sorts, this vehicle is really like a money fund, brokerage account, and checking account all rolled into one. As long as you keep a balance of $5,000–$10,000 in securities and cash, you can write as many free checks as you need. (Be sure to ask, however, whether you'll be subject to regular account charges, which can run as high as $125 annually.)

One such superb deal is available at the discount brokerage firm Charles Schwab. Customers who open up a Schwab One Account (800-421-4488) and make at least two trades a year can write unlimited checks on Schwab's interest-bearing savings account or money-market funds. Both options carry rates superior to your local bank's. Recently, for instance, Schwab was paying about 5%, or better than twice the national average. The Schwab One Account carries no maintenance fees, as long as you keep a monthly average balance of $5,000.

CYBERTIP

Bank Rate Monitor (http://www.bankrate.com) is the country's leading source for bank rates. Its Web page is a beauty, full of free information and calculations on bank rates, credit cards, and even banking trends. The outfit's excellent publications are also for sale at this site.

Get Higher Savings Yields

Bank savings accounts do have a sort of erstwhile appeal to them. Remember opening up yours in junior high or high school? And stashing your passbook in a secret drawer? Well, passbooks may be passé, but low savings yields—averaging 2.4% recently—are still in vogue at most banks. You'll do better if you consider the following:

• **Swap puny savings yields for money-market funds or accounts.** Surprise. The plumpest savings rates don't likely reside at your local bank. Two better ways to save are money-market funds (see page 71) and money-market accounts. Sure, the latter vehicle is handily available at your own bank. But you may be able to buttress your rate by as much as 2.5 additional percentage points by reaching out to a bank or savings and loan in another state. These accounts keep your money liquid and require only that you maintain a minimum balance—usually of $1,000 or more.

• **Scour the country for the best CD rates.** What's your bank paying on CDs? How about the bank down the street? Shop around your area all you like, but once again, you'll do even better by hiking out of town. The easiest way to canvas rates is to review *100 Highest Yields* (see phone number on page 71) or read the condensed rate information each month in **Money** magazine. If you find a rate out of state that is more favorable than what you get close to home, call to find out how to open an account—it's easy and certainly no more trouble than dealing with out-of-state credit card companies. (See the following box on buying CDs on the Web.) One caveat: Some out-of-state CDs have higher minimum deposits than those at your local bank.

Still prefer to stick with more familiar terrain? Then hunker down with your local bankers. As **Money** magazine discovered from a 1994 survey, a bank's advertised CD rate isn't carved in stone. For customers able to park a few thousand dollars into a CD, chances are roughly 40% that you can get a better rate—as much as a full percentage point higher—by merely asking or citing better deals elsewhere.

• **Before buying a CD, know which way interest rates are headed.** Are rates going up or down? The answer should dictate the term you seek when purchasing a CD. Generally you'll want to go with a short-term CD (six months to one year) when rates are rising. Once it matures, you may be able to grab a better rate. Buy a longer-term CD (one year or longer) when rates are declining, since you'll want to lock in at the highest likely rate for months to come.

CYBERTIP

Yes, you can shop for CDs even on the Web. Several highly rated institutions, accessible on-line, offer rich CD yields— and you don't need thousands to invest. Three worth checking out:

1st Source Bank (http://pawws.com/1stSrc_phtml/home.shtml). Its rates on six-month CDs were recently at 5.8%, for just a minimum of $500.
First Capital Bank (http://www.1stcapitalbk.com). A 12-month CD was recently available here at 5.9%, with a minimum deposit of $1,000.
Security First Network Bank (http://www.sfnb.com/infodesk/cd_info.html). A $1,500 minimum recently snared shoppers here a 5.9% yield.

Borrow—and Repay—Loans Smartly

By now you realize that you've got the power, and the leverage, as a good banking customer to cut bargains on everything from CD rates to banking fees. The same concept—getting banks to compete for your business—applies when you canvas the banking block for loans. Elsewhere in this book you'll find money-saving ideas for specific loans. (Later in this chapter, for instance, we'll tackle the most perilous type—the debt lurking on your credit cards. Chapter 2 covers auto loans; Chapter 7 primes you for college loans; and Chapter 1 takes up the topic of home mortgages and equity loans.) In the meantime, the following tips can boost your overall borrowing smarts.

• **Go for the shortest loan term possible.** As a rule, the shorter your loan term, the higher your monthly payments. The greater, too, are your loan savings. Take a traditional 30-year fixed-rate home mortgage. By halving the term to 15 years, you might increase your monthly payments by roughly 20%, but your total interest costs decline by about 50%. Consider a 15-year fixed-rate $100,000 loan at 7.75%, for instance, vs. a 30-year loan for the same amount at 8%. On the 15-year loan your total costs would be $69,430, or less than half of the $164,155 you'd owe for the 30-year loan.

• **Consider a loan's overall cost, not just the rate.** Interest rates are only part of the equation when figuring your loan's true cost. To size up your total debt burden, you'll need a laundry list of all fees and charges associated with the loan, such as origination fees, points, and application fees. Believe it or not, your lowest-rate option may actually be inferior to a higher-rate loan that carries fewer fees.

• **Secure a personal loan with a CD.** Many banks will give you more favorable loan terms if you pledge a certificate of deposit as collateral. By doing so, you may be entitled to a rate of only two to three percentage points above the CD rate. Recently that would have amounted to about 8%—or about half the rate of a typical unsecured personal loan.

• **Pay off your costliest debts first.** Think of this as a game of hot potato, prioritizing the highest, hottest loans. These are likely to include credit card debt and personal loans from your bank. You'll keep more money in your pocket by shedding high interest payments first and any tax-deductible loans (such as home-equity loans or margin account loans) dead last.

• **Check your credit report *before* your lender does.** Plan on dickering to get a point or two sliced off your loan rate? You'll want to be in fine form. Having followed our advice, you know how to gather rates of competing institutions. But you'll want even more artillery: your own credit report. Obtain a copy pronto, since any errors on this rap sheet could squelch your bargaining clout. Ask your prospective lenders which credit reporting agency they use (see below), then scan your report *a full two to three months prior to visiting lenders.* That way you'll have the chance to reverse any errors that undermine your application.
  Equifax: 800-685-1111
  TransUnion: 760 W. Sproul Rd., P.O. Box 390,
    Springfield, Pa. 19064
  TRW: 800-682-7654

• **Have loan payments deducted from your account automatically.** You'll save your lender any collection headaches—and yourself a few dollars in the process—by arranging to have all loan payments deducted automatically from your bank accounts. Assuming you bank at the institution that dispensed the loan, you can probably get at least a quarter point off your loan rate by going the automatic route.

PINCHING TIP

Pass on those mail "loans." Sooner or later you may open your mail to find an unsolicited check from your bank. Increasingly, banks are springing such surprises, of anywhere from $3,000 to $8,000, on customers. To many folks, they seem too good to be true. After all, endorsement and a deposit slip is all it takes to collect the cash. Rates on these loans, however, can be wrenchingly high. One bank in New Jersey, for instance, was recently charging 27%. With rates like that, your "loan" could rack up interest charges approaching 50% of the check amount.

Play the Credit Card Game to Win

Credit card hell. You've been there—that sordid place where your balances have run amok and the flames of debt burn relentlessly. While most of us need credit cards—to charge rental cars and airline tickets, etc., and to establish credit for other lenders—there's no need to get taken in the process. Here are eight ways to ease the pain of toting those plastic devils.

• **Use your savings to pay off plastic debt.** Mine your savings to retire credit card debt? You bet—it's common sense. With credit card rates topping 21% in some cases, there's no way to ensure a better return on your money than by paying off your credit card debt. The general rule: If your credit card rate tops the after-tax return you stand to make on, say, a bond or money fund, use your dough to pay off the plastic instead.

- **Chase the lowest rate and pay the lowest fees.** Credit card companies rack up billions in interest rates and annual fees. How much do you care to contribute? Your total credit card costs include two things: the interest rate (annual percentage rate, or APR) and the annual fees. Since these figures vary widely, you'd be wise to shop around, especially out of state. But first, it's helpful to assess your charging habits. Do you make your payments in full, each and every month, or do you routinely carry a balance (known as revolving)?

If you pay in full each month, pesky interest charges won't have time to sneak up on you. Therefore, *reach for a card that carries no annual fee and offers a grace period*. By getting that float of up to 25 days between when you receive your bill and when payment is due, you effectively get a free 25-day loan each month. Of course, you should also seek out a card with a below average APR (anything under 18%, for example), for those occasional times when you need to revolve.

If you carry a balance, on the other hand, those three key initials—APR—*should be your number one concern*. Here's how just a few percentage points can affect your annual charges. Let's assume you carry an average monthly balance of $2,500. If your card has an APR of 14%, you'll pay about $350 in finance charges each year. Get suckered into an APR of 18%, on the other hand, and you'll shell out $450 in finance charges during that same year—or $100 more.

Plenty of issuers offer reasonable APRs (see box on pages 82–83). Bear in mind, you'll need a pristine credit report to snare the very best rates. For the privilege of a low APR (as lean as 9% in some cases) expect to pay an annual fee of at least $25, but not more than $50.

- **Avoid the "minimum payment" trap.** Card issuers push those "minimum" payments for a reason. Usually about

2.5% of your total balance, they sure seem tempting (after all, 2.5% of a $1,000 bill is just $25). Don't buckle. That pittance of a payment is setting you up for interest rate backlash.

Assume you owe $1,000 on a credit card charging 17%. If you were to pay the lowest amount due each month, it would take you *12* years to pay off the balance in full. Your total interest payments? A scalding $979, or nearly as much as your original bill (for a detailed example, see table "How Paying the 'Minimum Amount Due' Does Maximum Damage," page 80).

What if you have big plastic debts piled up but can't afford to slay the balance in one or two chunks? This is a likely scenario, since fully 70% of all credit card holders carry over an average balance each month of $1,700. Believe it or not, recovery won't require a 12-Step program. *By paying just $15 to $20 per month above the minimum balance, you can wipe out your debt two to three times faster* than handing over the lowest amount due.

To help you plan a plastic payoff, the consumer group BankCard Holders of America (see box below) has a neat solution. Its $15 Debt Zapper program prioritizes your card payments and shows you exactly how long it will take to retire your plastic debt. The package also comes with a list of low-interest/no-annual-fee credit cards.

BankCard Holders of America (BHA) is a nonprofit group dedicated to helping consumers use credit cards wisely. BHA's personalized Debt Zapper reports ($15) will assess all your credit card debts and suggest a payment strategy for erasing them faster. For more information, contact BHA at 524 Branch Dr. Salem, Va. 24153; or phone 540-389-5445.

HOW PAYING THE "MINIMUM AMOUNT DUE" DOES MAXIMUM DAMAGE

Okay, so you've binged a bit over the holidays, charging up $2,869 on gifts. *Don't even think* about skirting your debt by paying just the minimum amount due, typically 2.5% of your balance. Your sentence for such folly, assuming an average APR of 18.22%? A nasty $3,433 in interest charges, and a grueling *14 years* to settle the debt. To the poor consumer who chooses such a route, the following table shows the original and after-interest costs of those Christmas list items.

GIFT	PRICE PAID	FINAL COST, AFTER INTEREST
Briefcase	$258	$567
Theater tickets	$101	$221
Computer	$2,149	$4,731
CDs	$50	$109
Lingerie	$90	$193
Pen set	$129	$280
Cuff links	$70	$153
Teddy bear	$22	$48
TOTAL	$2,869	$6,302

• **Carry only one or two cards.** Most Americans get between three and four unsolicited credit card mailings per week—you know, preapproved this, and low-introductory-rate that. Sure, the average consumer totes several cards. But most consumers really need only one or two. Adhering to such a plastic diet saves you money the old-fashioned way, by forcing you to pay your balance each month (as the American Express card demands) or by limiting your available credit line (if you carry one Visa or Mastercard).

• **Transfer your balances to a lower rate card.** There are two ways to shuffle your credit balances profitably. The first and by far the better method is to *get approved for a low-fixed-rate card.* In many instances this will allow you to transfer thousands of high-rate plastic debt to the new lower rate and save big on finance charges. If you were to transfer $1,500 from your 21% card to another with a rate of 13%, for example, you could save close to $100 in interest over a 12-month period. The second method is a bit more daring. This involves dumping debts on a so-called teaser rate card, then retiring the balance before the teaser rate expires. (See "teaser rates," page 82.)

• **Don't forget your credit union's card.** Here's yet another example of how credit unions outshine banks. Their credit cards work just like anybody else's, but customers get a big break on rates. The average credit union card carries an APR of just 13% vs. an average of 18% for bank cards. Bear in mind that you will not read about credit union credit cards on lists such as *Bank Rate Monitor's*, so try to finagle membership where you can.

• **Get a fee break for the asking.** Assuming you boast a solid payment history, and have held your card for a year or more, many issuers will simply eliminate your $15–$50 annual fee. Just ask. With card issuers slugging it out to gain new customers, many are in a favorable negotiating mood. The best candidates for a rate reduction are customers in good standing who pay stinging APRs—anywhere above the national average of 18%. A call to the card's customer service division, alerting them to better offers you've received, could skim anywhere from two to five percentage points off your rate. Depending on the card balance, you'd potentially save hundreds in a single year.

• **Use "teaser rates" to your benefit.** Two-thirds of all credit card offers today hype so-called teaser rates—tempting rock-bottom APRs of around 6%. The real drill, of course, goes something like this: The issuer lets you enjoy low-rate heaven for six to 12 months. After that, rates climb higher than Jack's beanstalk, usually no less than 17%. Disciplined types can turn teasers to their advantage, though. Use the card (by charging fresh or transferring higher-rate balances from other cards) for as long as the low rate applies. Before the rate hike kicks in, snip it in two and cancel the account. By the time you do so, you'll likely have other teaser offers idling in your mailbox, giving you the chance to start all over again.

CREDIT CARD "DEALS" THAT ARE ACTUALLY DUPES

If, like the average American, you receive more than three credit card solicitations in the mail each week, you may be blindsided by the so-called deals that many tout. Watch out. Nasty card features like the three outlined below will end up costing you.

1. *Variable-rate cards.* Many issuers pitch variable-rate cards (whose interest rates fluctuate) as a way to save dough. But the rates on these cards usually gyrate upward, not downward. Why? Because most of them carry "minimum" rates—APRs that you'll find buried in the fine print of their ads. One large bank was recently offering a Visa card at a rate of prime plus 9%, for a total APR of roughly 17% at the time. That's not too

---

bad, coming in at a shade below the national average card rate. But hold on. The card's "minimum" rate is 18.9%. This is yet another lesson on why it pays to read the fine print.

2. *Bogus no-fee cards.* Just above we outlined why a card with no annual fee and a low APR is the best of all possible plastic worlds. Creative banking marketers, however, have come up with at least a product or two that nixes any potential savings. For example, one card we found seems attractive at first glimpse, with a low APR and no fee. There was just one hitch. When signing up, customers must agree to take out a cash advance of $2,000 or more, at the onerous interest rate of 22%. Over a 12-month period, such a loan would cost customers close to $450 in interest charges.

3. *Payment protection plans.* Some card companies are out to scare you, literally, into paying for worthless features. What if you were to become disabled or unemployed? That's the pitch of one of the most commonly hyped card "protection" plans. It claims to cover a customer's balance in the event of such a catastrophe. But despite their high cost (about $7 for each $100 on your balance, or $14 per month on a $2,000 balance), these plans give Band-Aid protection. Most (surprise!) cover just your minimum monthly payment.

CYBERTIP

An awesome resource for personal finance queries, the Financenter Website (http://www.financenter.com) contains pointed advice and worksheets for all types of borrowers. You'll be amazed at the site's built-in calculators, which, among other feats, let you customize payment loan scenarios (such as how long it will take you to pay off your credit card debts).

CHAPTER 5

Smart Ways to Save When You Invest

All investors, of course, want their dollars to flourish. Bringing up a lush portfolio, though, requires more than just picking the right stocks, bonds, and mutual funds. To get the highest returns possible, you'll need to get smart about your investment expenses—the money you pay to keep your portfolio up and running.

Tempted by a sizzling new mutual fund? Watch out. It just may carry a brutal sales load, or commission—a fee that crashes your earning power. Ogling individual stocks or maybe U.S. Treasury bonds? Again, doing so without an eye on fees is unwise. And what about those shares you want to sell at Bill Gates profits? Tick tick tick. That's the sound of the tax bomb that awaits when you redeem.

Fact is, everyone on the investment block—from broker to tax man to mutual fund manager—wants to earn money not just for you, but *on* you as well. Outsmart them and save up to 40% on your investment expenses.

The Tax-Deferred Savings Plan: You've Got to Be in It to Win It

Bet you can't think of many folks who would pass up free money. How about free money *and* a tax break? Nobody's that foolish, right? Wrong. Each year millions of Americans forgo a sterling opportunity to invest their hard-earned dollars cheaply—through their employers' tax-deferred savings plans. The most common such plan is the 401(k), named for its place in the tax code; others include 457s (mainly for public employees) and 403(b)s (for workers at nonprofits).

With a 401(k) employees can direct a set sum from their paychecks (up to $9,500 in 1996) into a variety of options, such as stocks, mutual funds, or money-market accounts. Because the money is deducted *before taxes,* each dollar contributed helps lower your taxable income. As a bonus, most companies kick in matching dollars (yes, free money)—of about 50 cents for every buck you put in, up to about 2% of your salary. Contributions, and all earnings, grow tax-deferred, meaning you won't pay taxes as long as it remains untouched. (For all the advice you'll ever need on 401(k)s, check another book in the *MONEY: America's Financial Advisor Series: Take Charge of Your Future,* by Eric Schurenberg.)

• **Invest the maximum in your 401(k) and win big.** Many people err by raking scant dollars into their 401(k) plans, then shoveling additional cash into other investments. A better idea is to maximize your tax-deferred options first, since you get the double Dutch treat of free money and a federal tax reduction.

Not swooning yet? Here's how tax-deferred savings gives your money legs. Over just a one-year period a person in the 28% tax bracket placing $6,000 of her salary into a 401(k) account *saves $1,450 a year in taxes.* Pretty good, and it only gets better over the long haul. So now consider a 30-year-old with a $60,000 salary. If she were to save 6% of her pay each year, earning 8% in a fully taxable account, she'd amass roughly $186,000 by age 60. Sounds impressive *until* you realize that had that same woman invested an identical sum in a *tax-deferred account,* her stash upon her sixty-fifth birthday would be an impressive $408,000.

If you can't yet afford to shell out the maximum contribution, that's okay—you'll get there. In the meantime, aim to set aside no less than what's required to get your employer's full matching contribution.

• **Fund an IRA.** For those without access to a tax-deferred plan at work, a good alternative is the individual retirement account (IRA). Though not as generous as its 401(k) cousin, the IRA still lets you deduct some or all of your contribution ($2,000 per year or $2,250 for single-income couples) from your federal tax bill.

Even if you can't fund a deductible IRA, consider funneling that two grand into a *nondeductible IRA.* Your money still gets special treatment in such a vehicle, since its earnings grow untainted by taxes until withdrawal. (Presumably, when you remove the money you'll be in a different, lower tax bracket.)

Lower Your Mutual Fund Investing Costs

Just 10 years ago the average American barely ventured into the stock market. What a difference a decade makes, with investors today pouring billions into over 5,300 stock and bond funds—a 350% increase over 1986. Buying shares in a mutual fund, of course, is a lot less risky than purchasing individual stocks. That's because funds, depending on their objectives, invest in many stocks, across several industries. The ups and downs of any one company, then, won't likely make or break a fund's performance.

Selecting the "right" mutual funds for you depends on many things: your own tolerance for risk (just like the stock and bond markets, fund performance will be up and down); your short- and long-term financial needs (the stock market, even via funds, isn't the place to be if you need your money back in less than five years); and, naturally, your own budget (some funds require a minimum initial investment of $1,000 or more). One important common denominator for all fund investors, however, is cost. Since you will likely encounter a smorgasbord of fees and expenses, make it your business to keep them as low as possible.

• **Choose no-loads.** To the uninitiated, "no-load" might sound like some newfangled offering at the gas pump. Well, almost. This type of fund, in "mutual fund–speak," is simply one that charges no "load," or sales commission. Your entry is free. More than one-third of all stock mutual funds sold today are no-loads. Buying them is easy. Simply request information on the fund by dialing the fund company's toll-free number, and mail your check.

The other, less gallant variety of funds does carry loads, charging investors anywhere from 1% to 9% in sales commissions. Typically these are sold by brokers, insurance agents, or financial planners, who will help you choose which funds to buy and advise you when to dump them. So how might this "load vs. no-load" proposition affect your money? A $5,000 investment, for instance, placed in a no-load fund gets you rolling with precisely $5,000. That same sum poured into a fund with a typical 4% load buys you shares worth just $4,800.

Don't assume that loaded funds perform better than no-loads. There's no evidence to suggest this at all. So why bother with them? Some people will pay a load simply for the benefit of a broker's advice. Keep in mind, however, that millions of fund investors make informed decisions about buying and selling shares on their own. You will do better as a mutual fund investor, in fact, by doing some homework of your own: raise your financial IQ by reading publications like **MONEY** magazine and your newspaper's business section on a regular basis; also scour a mutual fund's prospectus to understand its objective, performance history, and fee structure. Basic steps like these will help you to make sound investment choices.

That said, there are several fund families that offer a healthy selection (more than 10 apiece) of no-load stock funds.

```
Dreyfus.....................................................800-645-6561
Fidelity.....................................................800-544-8888
Invesco.....................................................800-525-8085
Montgomery.............................................800-572-3863
Scudder.....................................................800-225-2470
Strong ......................................................800-368-1030
Twentieth Century....................................800-345-2021
T. Rowe Price...........................................800-638-5660
Vanguard..................................................800-662-7447
Wright Managed Investment Companies.............800-888-9471
```

• **Look for low expenses and administrative fees.** It's easy enough to avoid a load. Unfortunately, though, fund investors can't escape fees altogether. After all, money managers don't work for free. Fund investors pay them handsomely—in part through a fund's annual expenses.

On a yearly basis, the average domestic stock mutual fund charges about 1.3% to keep things humming (1% for taxable bond funds and 0.75% for a muni bond fund). This percentage will be spelled out in the fund prospectus, under the column headed "Expense Ratio." Expect to pay slightly above average expenses for aggressive growth stocks (closer to 2%) and foreign stocks (about 1.75%). Otherwise, consider anything in the 2% and over range excessive. You can almost surely find another fund that will perform just as well for less money.

One expense you should try to sidestep entirely is the nasty 12b-1 fee. As imperceptible as a tsetse fly, this one bites investors each and every year. Worst of all, the fee is for stuff you shouldn't be paying for, like marketing and distribution costs. Avoid the 12b-1 sting by calling a fund's 800 number and asking, point-blank, if you will be subject to one. If the answer is "yes," take your money elsewhere.

• **Consider funds that are easy on your tax bill.** Mutual fund investors bite nails over performance, looking at last month's results, last year's performance, even last week's turn of events. There's another performance barometer that often goes unnoticed, however. Homing in on a fund's likely tax liability can save you a bundle.

If your fund has a high turnover—if, in other words, it buys and sells shares very often—it will likely realize frequent capital gains. Such activity keeps the door ajar for the tax man—and can be a bummer to your overall return. When comparing two relatively similar funds, then, go for the one with the lower turnover ratio. This information is readily available by dialing the fund's toll-free account line.

By using sophisticated timing techniques, some fund managers can be active traders and still minimize taxes. So another important tax clue lies in a fund's *tax-efficiency rating*. This barometer, expressed as a percentage, measures the amount of a fund's total return left after taxes. A grade of 80% or better signals a tax champ. (As an example, when **MONEY** magazine publishes its annual fund rankings, a particular fund might rank tenth when measured by total returns alone. By factoring in a high tax-efficiency ratio, though, a fund could easily soar in the listings from, say, tenth place to third.)

To find this data, scour the mutual fund tables as published in most personal finance magazines and newspapers. Also ask a fund's customer service representatives if one of your selections has a specific policy to ease shareholders' tax burdens.

• **Join an extended fund family with a discount brokerage.** "All in the family" does have a certain ring to it, even when applied to mutual fund investing. On that note, it pays to consider the fund offerings of discount brokerage firms. Several, including Fidelity Investments, Charles Schwab, and Jack White, let you invest under an umbrella of dozens of fund families, giving you one-stop access to hundreds of no-load funds—all for free.

As long as you have a regular brokerage account (see the discussion of discount brokers, pages 93–94), these firms will hold and manage your mutual fund accounts gratis. You can thank the mutual fund companies for their generosity on this score. They pick up the tab for servicing your account, an expense they more than recoup from the piles of new cash flowing in through such handy channels.

Aside from gaining access to multiple fund families, shareholders get other goodies, too: the brokerage firm will forward your funds' annual reports and proxy statements to you and in some cases will toss in a comprehensive newsletter covering all funds available.

Another benefit is that the sheer rapidity of these programs saves you dough. Since transactions generally take place the same day, your money works literally around the clock. If you were to transfer dollars between different funds by mail, you'd lose several days due to shipping and processing. That, of course, costs you time and money.

Keep in mind that because these firms intend to encourage long-term investing, most charge customers for making more than three or four fund redemptions per year. The lowest-cost nationwide programs include the following:

Fidelity's FundsNetwork, which gives you access to more than 400 no-load mutual funds. Four free redemptions per year.

Schwab's OneSource has over 500 no-load funds. It allows you to sell funds without penalty as long as you hold the shares for at least 90 days.

Waterhouse Securities has 354 no-load funds. It permits five free short-term redemptions (holding six months or less) within a one-year period.

• If you have little to invest, try dollar-cost averaging. Sure, it's a mouthful. But dollar-cost averaging is actually quite simple. Hence its beauty: shell out a set amount each month, say, $50 toward a stock mutual fund. During market lulls (when share prices are low) your set sum buys more shares, while during peak cycles (when prices are high), you get fewer. Thus you're virtually assured of scooping up shares at a fair average price every time.

There's another advantage to this painless investing tactic. Most mutual fund companies will zap your contributions from your bank account gratis. In fact, by doing so, the majority of companies will also let you bypass any minimum investment rules. Have a hankering to get in the Fidelity Advisor, which carries a $2,500 minimum initial investment? By dollar-cost averaging, you'll be ushered in for any sum over $50—as long as you set up that automatic withdrawal plan.

• Use cheap-to-own index funds in place of large company funds and bond funds. Have a fetish for large company, AKA large-cap, stocks? What about taxable bonds? Chances are you do, or you will, since most financial pros recommend peppering your portfolio with anywhere between 20% and 30% of big company stocks (like AT&T, Exxon, and General Electric) and from 15% to 45% bonds.

Take your pick—plenty of mutual funds offer a savory mix of either. But they'll cost you. The average large company stock fund carries an expense ratio of about 1.3% annually and perhaps a load, or commission, to boot. Likewise, bond funds are saddled with some of the steepest expenses in the business. A smarter, cheaper way to bulk up on these vehicles is to *tap into low-cost index funds,* which tend to perform better, and charge less for the privilege, than funds that specialize in them.

Put simply, autopilotlike index funds are designed to mirror the performance of major market indices (these include the Standard & Poor's 500 Stock Index and the Lehman Brothers Aggregate Bond Index). Large-cap index funds, such as Vanguard's Index 500, do so like champs, returning more to investors than other plain-vanilla large-cap funds. Similarly, taxable bond index funds tend to hurtle other bond funds. Best of all, *they cost less to own.* Vanguard, for example, charges a piddly 0.19% expense ratio for its index funds, compared with an average of 1.3% for other large-cap funds; on the bond side, its Total Bond Market Fund asks just 0.2% a year, stacked against the average taxable bond fund take of 1%.

Save When You Buy (and Sell) Stocks and Bonds

So you want to move beyond mutual funds and buy some individual stock. Maybe just a single share to adorn your safe-deposit box. Go ahead—reach out to a full-service brokerage firm such as Merrill Lynch or Prudential, and ouch! The commission ax will come down to sever a few digits—of the numeric sort, we mean. According to financial counselors Mercer Inc., the average broker commission was recently $246. That's fine for folks who don't mind getting fleeced. Others, of course, may prefer the lower commission charged by *discount brokers.*

That's right. Assuming you've done your own homework—which shares you'd like to pick up and which ones you care to dump—a discount broker can save you more than 70%. We say "know your stuff" because discounters, by definition, cut out all service frills such as offering advice on specific trades. Most have offices you can visit (where you can pick up information on various products and execute trades). But aside from their toll-free phone staffs, which dispense very basic information about products and fees, customers of discount brokers are largely on their own.

With 232 branches in 47 states, the largest discount broker, Charles Schwab, charges about $40, or a quarter the price of their full-service competitors. Other discounters include Jack White, Fidelity, and Quick & Reilly. Each of these discounters will rise to the occasion of dispensing research and/or advice if you ask—for a fee.

Cheaper still are so-called deep discounters. The bargain-basement traders in their field, these phone-only shops, including Pacific Brokerage Services and Kennedy, Cabot, command as little as half of regular discounters. Before you head to them, however, know that you stand to get virtually no other service than straightforward trades. No extras, not even for a fee. So you'd better be confident in your trading abilities.

• **Invest on-screen.** For those who make several trades per year, using discounters' on-line programs can *save another 10%*. Place electronic stock trades round the clock with Charles Schwab's *StreetSmart* software. Schwab had been advertising the kit for $39. But if you walk into any Schwab branch, they will give you the package (Macintosh and Windows versions) *for free*. The software also has a 24-hour support line (which can also be accessed for free on the Web at http://www.schwab.com). Fidelity's *On-line Xpress* also gives you the 10% discount edge, but for a price. Their software package (for DOS or Windows only) costs $49.95, plus $7.50 shipping. Call 800-544-9375.

CYBERTIP

It didn't take long for the deepest of deep discounters to sur-
face on-line, with a vengeance. Flaunting superslim trading
costs of $12 to $45 per transaction, these Website services
can save you more than 80% off the price of conventional
trades. For example, E*Trade (http://www.etrade.com) charges
$14.95–$19.95 per trade and requires an opening account balance of just $1,000. Similar sites include Accutrade
(www.accutrade.com), Ceres Securities (www.ceres.com), and
Pacific Brokerage Services (www.tradepbs.com).

• **Tap into DRIPs and no-load stocks.** For those
tempted by individual equities, but dogged by shallow pockets,
there exist two good, affordable ways to ease into the stock
market. Both of the methods focus on cutting out the middleman (the broker) and let you buy shares directly from participating companies.

DRIPs. Don't be fooled by the name. Dividend reinvest-
ment plans (DRIPs) are among corporate America's smartest—
and most benevolent—inventions. Nearly 1,000 publicly traded
companies now offer them. Here's how they work.

After you purchase one share of stock—just one—through
the usual channels (your broker, that is), participating companies
will allow you to buy additional shares directly, often for free.
You can even pad your account, in many cases, with fractional
shares, investing as little as $10 at a time on a weekly or
monthly basis. As their name implies, DRIPs put your invested
dividends to work, buying even more shares. The best plans
even give you a discount of 3% to 5% when you scoop up
shares this way. An excellent source for learning more about
DRIP plans is the *DRIP Investor* ($59 for the first year; call 219-
852-3220 for subscriptions).

Direct purchase plans, or "no-load stocks." The next genera-
tion following DRIPs, so-called no-load stocks, go even one

better. You need not buy that first share from a broker. Cutting out the middleman entirely, they permit investors to buy into a company as they would a mutual fund. Just send in a check for a minimum of anywhere from $25 to $2,000, and your money buys as many shares and/or fractional shares as the day's closing price permits. Thereafter you may make additional cash payments to your account, and in most cases you can use your reinvested dividends to buy more shares.

Since January of 1995, when the Securities and Exchange Commission made it easier for companies to launch these programs, "no-load" stock plans have taken off, with the roster of companies offering them rocketing by 80% from mid-1995 to mid-1996. At press time there were 122 such programs up and running, with blue chips like McDonald's, Procter & Gamble, and Exxon adding luster to the list. A free service, set up by the folks at the *DRIP Investor*, makes it easy to get information on this rapidly expanding universe. The Direct Stock Purchase Plan Clearinghouse (800-774-4117) is a 24-hour automated service that will take your order for information kits on as many as five no-load stocks per call. As of this writing, the clearinghouse had signed up 30 companies for its service

• **Consider your tax burden when buying and selling stocks.** Shareholders can win big in the stock market, only to have the grim tax reaper hatchet their gains. Over the past 10 years, for example, the average stock investor sacrificed 12% of his/her money to taxes.

Though Congress may see fit to tame capital-gains rates (or even implement a flat tax), the IRS wants its fair share in the meantime. Investors should not let tax concerns hold their investing style hostage, of course. The following three tips can save most stockholders money by deferring and/or reducing taxes.

1. Place any income stocks in your tax-deferred account. Because your tax-favored IRA or 401(k) gives you a natural tax advantage, you'll want to place the biggest tax monster stocks there.

Best candidates: income stocks (such as utilities, financial services companies, and an array of blue chips), whose often hefty dividends would ordinarily be taxed each and every year. By stashing income stocks in your IRA or other tax-deferred account, you get to hold off paying taxes until withdrawal (ideally at age 62 or later).

2. When you sell stock, dump your costliest shares first. Do you own, say, 100 shares of General Electric that you purchased over the past four years? Not all of them, as you probably guessed, were created equal. Sure, any profit you've made will trigger taxes. But by selling those shares for which you paid the most, you'll minimize your tax bill.

PINCHING TIP

Are you overpaying for growth stocks? A company's p/e ratio gives the story best. This handy fraction, called the *price/earnings ratio,* indicates when a stock is overpriced, or overvalued, relative to the rest of the market. If the market's average p/e is at 15, for instance, and a stock you're considering weighs in with a p/e of 20, it's probably a questionable deal. You can arrive at a stock's p/e by dividing the share price by its earnings per share.

• **Buy U.S. Treasuries direct from Uncle Sam.** Would you hand over money to pay a bridge toll if there was a "cross for free" lane? Definitely not. Which is why it makes no sense whatsoever to buy Treasuries—we're talking U.S. Treasury bills, notes, and bonds—through a broker. Sure, your friendly broker or discount broker will be happy to sell you these instruments, for anywhere from $30 to $100.

For the price of a stamp you can buy Treasuries direct from the U.S. government. To get rolling on your own, you need just $1,000 to invest. Contact one of the Federal Reserve Bank's 37 branches nationwide (see your phone book or write to Bureau of Public Debt, Washington, D.C. 20239). You'll want to request an application for a Treasury Direct account.

• **Avoid bond purchases on the secondary market.** Although most items sold "secondhand" go for less than their original asking price, this is not so in the bond market. Original bond issues, sold through underwriters on the primary market, generally carry no sales charges. And everybody—from small-fry investors to institutional bigwigs—pays the same price. That egalitarian scenario changes drastically down the line, when these issues are hawked by brokers on the secondary market. By then a fair market value may be difficult to determine; and the price you pay is apt to be higher than preferred rates for big institutional buyers. You're also sure to pay a brokerage commission. To get in the game more cheaply, be sure to ask your broker about new (or original) corporate and municipal issues.

Get the Best Investment Advice for the Least Money

Who's minding your dough? You are, you say? Why then, you've got it all figured out: a college savings kitty for the kids, an oiled and lubed retirement plan, and enough insurance to take care of your loved ones in the unfortunate event of your early demise.

Okay, maybe you *could* use some help. Assuming any of these issues have been vexing your pocketbook, and that your household income is $85,000 or more, you could probably profit from more than just a calculator and a pile of financial magazines.

A financial adviser can take the bits and pieces of your unruly financial life and transform them into a masterful plan that works. Though you'll pay smartly for their services, *a good planner's advice can save you many times over the amount you pay them in fees.* The challenge from your end is to find one who suits your needs—someone you can afford *and trust.* Don't be easily impressed by someone calling himself (or herself) a financial planner. These days that title is tossed about as freely as "personal trainer," with more than 300,000 people in the United States claiming the role. Because this free-for-all industry is loosely regulated, and credentials are often squishy, you should choose an adviser carefully, perhaps seeking referrals from friends or colleagues.

Most reputable planners will offer you a free introductory session. Beyond that, their services aren't cheap. As a rule, financial planners are categorized by the way in which they get paid.

The most holistic way to go, in general, is with *fee-only planners.* These are advisers who dispense their wisdom for an hourly fee (anywhere from $75 to $250) or a percentage (1%–4%) of the assets you ask them to manage. For an additional sum of about $1,000–$4,000, they'll also craft a written, long-term financial plan tackling everything from estate planning to tax reduction. The boon with this stripe of planner has to do with their relative impartiality: fee-only planners sell no investments, so they don't stand to profit from steering you to one investment choice over another.

Next are *fee and commission planners.* As the name implies, they earn money two ways: from commissions on products they sell (such as life insurance and stocks) and from fees for services rendered. Like fee-only planners, they may charge a separate sum to draft a comprehensive written plan.

The wolves of the pack are *commission-only planners,* whose very title suggests that their biggest interest may be in loading you up with high-commission products. Though they appear in many guises, commission-only types are most likely to be found at full-service brokerage houses such as Merrill Lynch and Prudential.

As we said earlier, planners typically offer an introductory meeting, for about 30 minutes, at no charge. The purpose is to get a fix on your needs, but it's also your chance to *ask them lots of questions* (like, How much do you charge? and, How has your track record fared?) and to request a sample financial plan (with the names blocked out) of two or three clients similar to you.

If you can't afford the ongoing assistance of a planner, consider a miniplan that may cost you $300–$1,000. Many fee-only planners provide one-shot plans that show clients how to solve a specific problem, such as how to save for college or retirement.

Two good sources for finding reputable planners:

The Institute of Certified Financial Planners (ICFP) has a membership comprising all three types of planners. To be listed as a member, practitioners must have passed a battery of tests on investments and finance, earning them the well-regarded designation of CFP (for certified financial planner). Contact the organization at 800-282-7526 to locate a CFP in your area.

The National Association of Personal Financial Advisors (NAPFA) has a membership of 250 fee-only planners. Most are CFPs. Call 888-FEE-ONLY for a list of planners in your area. NAPFA also provides a free checklist of questions to help you select the right planner for your needs.

And . . . a Pearl of a Savings Strategy for Real Estate Investors

SWAP A PIECE OF REAL ESTATE, TAX-FREE

Got an investment property (such as a small apartment building) to unload, but recoil at the tax tab staring you down? Try a neat deal called *like-kind exchange*. Among the most overlooked tax breaks on the books, this gem lets investors swap one property for another and—get this—escape any capital-gains taxes. Yup. All taxes are deferred until you sell, if you ever do. A brief rundown:

Let's assume you have a four-unit rental you want to sell. You also wish to acquire another, similar property. To defer taxes, you wish to execute a "like-kind" exchange. There are four players in this scenario: you (the exchanger), the buyer (of your old property), the seller (of the new property you acquire), and an intermediary. In abbreviated fashion, this is how the deal works (this example assumes that the properties being swapped are of equal value):

1. First, you locate a *buyer* for your property.
2. You hand over your property deed to an *intermediary* (such as an attorney or even a friend), who will help the deal move along.
3. Rather than pay you directly, the buyer of your property pays the intermediary. You now have 45 days to locate a new property to acquire (if you haven't already done so).
4. When you've located a new property to acquire (you have 180 days from the time the money changes hands between intermediary and buyer), the intermediary pays the *seller* and you collect the deed for the new property.
5. Eureka! You are the proud owner of a new property, owing no tax on the real estate you just swapped. Serious swappers

should check out John T. Reed's *Aggressive Tax Avoidance for Real Estate Investors* (to order, call 800-635-5425).

CYBERTIP

Visit Money Online (http://www.moneymag.com). Our Pathfinder site, updated daily, is packed with the latest investment wisdom and trends. Count on this site to help you collect cutting-edge savings on mutual funds, stocks, bonds, and loads more.

CHAPTER 6

Take a Scalpel to All Your Medical Expenses

Even if you boast a sterling health policy, chances are better than 50-50 that you'll have to foot at least some of your family's medical bills out-of-pocket. With health care expenditures rising 60% faster than inflation, and consuming 14% of the nation's gross domestic product, the diagnosis is clear: no family can afford to sit back and be passive about health care costs.

- Fact: Within any given city, doctor fees for the same service can vary by as much as 733%.
- Fact: Nearly 25% of all medical procedures performed each year are unnecessary, costing Americans $6 billion to $18 billion annually.
- The Medicare hospital trust fund, the elderly's biggest "insurance" source, is slated to go broke by the year 2002.

Jolting statistics like that make the best case for being a smart, and informed, medical consumer. Put simply, you'll need to get more aggressive about comparing prices and services— even challenging costs.

Fortunately all of this is getting easier. As health care continues to grab national headlines and top politicians' agendas, consumer information on medical care and costs is only a phone call, or an Internet connection, away. In several cities, including Atlanta, Boston, Pittsburgh, and St. Louis, the newsstand publication *Health Pages* breaks out fees for area medical providers, from doctors to insurance companies. On the Internet, Web browsers can tap into numerous medical Websites (see page 107) for a virtual library of health studies, treatment information, and price projections. Care to call to compare doctors' fees? One good dial-in source is the Health Care Cost Hotline (800-383-3434), which for a nominal charge sends you median fee information for doctors and dentists in your city.

Before spending another cent on medical care, consider these other cost-cutting remedies for what ails you.

HALVE YOUR MEDICAL INSURANCE COSTS THE EASY WAY

Here's a guaranteed way to lower your family's health insurance premiums. Simply raise your health insurance deductible—the amount you must pay out-of-pocket before benefits kick in—and watch the savings flow. Many plans, for instance, call for a $500 deductible. By doubling that amount to $1,000, however, the average family of four might have recently cut their premiums in half, from $4,000 to $2,000 a year. (For more details about all types of insurance savings, turn to Chapter 8.)

If the thought of meeting that higher deductible gives you panic attacks, try an easy antidote. Set aside some of the money you save on premiums—about $160 per month in the example above—to pay those up-front bills. Or adjust your flexible spending account to cover most out-of-pocket costs (see FSAs, below).

USE AN FSA TO PAY JUST $600 FOR $1,000 WORTH OF MEDICAL BILLS

Helping employees to take a bite out of medical expenses, roughly 53% of all large companies offer so-called flexible spending accounts (FSAs). These plans let employees tuck away pretax dollars to pay for a range of unreimbursed medical costs (see list below). If your company makes this type of plan available to you, sign up ASAP to reap healthy tax savings. Let's say, for instance, that your family spends about $1,000 for uncovered medical bills each year. Pay with your regular bank savings and you'll owe exactly $1,000. But by using money stashed in an FSA—remember, those dollars have been untainted by federal, Social Security, and in some cases state taxes—a family in the 28% tax bracket would save about $400.

Most employees can annually contribute between $2,000 and $5,000 to an FSA. The money is painlessly deducted from your paycheck in equal installments, before taxes. Best of all, your account need not be fully funded for you to withdraw the entire amount pledged. Big expenses, therefore, are covered at any point in the year.

There's one caveat to these plans, which can be as cruel as they are kind: You must use every cent in your FSA by year-end. Otherwise you lose it. You can avoid such waste by budgeting just the right amount in your FSA. Before enrolling, dig out your medical records from previous years and make a tally of health expenditures for 12 months ahead. Use your projections to figure how much you must set aside. The following are allowable expenses for FSAs:

- deductibles (the amount you pay out-of-pocket for health care before your insurance benefits kick in)
- prescription eyewear
- alternative health treatments, such as acupuncture
- dependent care (see below)
- transportation to and from medical appointments

- prescribed medical devices, such as vaporizers and orthopedic supports

SAVE ALMOST $1,000 PER CHILD BY PAYING DAY CARE COSTS WITH AN FSA

Come April 15, many families bask in the generosity of Uncle Sam's child care credit. As far as the tax code goes, it's a pretty decent gesture, saving hundreds for the average couple with an adjusted gross income of up to $28,000. If you can choose between using an FSA and the child care credit (sorry, you can't have both), an FSA is clearly the better deal.

How's that? The child care credit gets stingier and stingier as your income rises. Once your adjusted gross income hits $28,000, you can take only 20% of the $720 per-child credit. The FSA, on the other hand, is designed to pump bigger and better tax savings as your income soars. By paying for child care with an FSA, a couple earning over $48,000 would save as much as $1,400 on one child's care per year, assuming both spouses contribute the maximum to an FSA.

CHOOSE AN HMO AND SPEND 80% LESS ON HEALTH CARE

These days most employers let workers select from two or three different medical plans. Invariably the roster will contain two or more *managed care options,* which by definition limit patients to a specific universe of doctors.

Is that so bad? Not necessarily. Compared with the traditional fee for service plans—which permit visits to any doctor or specialist and reimburse up to 80%—managed care programs can save you money without giving up too much quality. There are two types: preferred provider organizations (PPOs) and health maintenance organizations (HMOs). PPOs are the more flexible of the pair, allowing visits to doctors outside their fixed network. HMOs, by contrast, offer the healthiest savings. A family of four, for instance, stands to save as much as 80% a year by opting for an HMO over a fee-for-service plan because HMOs have no significant costs aside from the premiums. There are no deductibles, and they cover both preventive care and annual physical exams.

Granted, it wasn't too long ago that HMOs were like the Yugos of all medical plans. Their tight selection of doctors, mainly, gave them a bad rep. Today, however, surveys by the American Medical Association confirm that nearly 80% of active physicians are signed on with at least one HMO or PPO network. The result: HMO quality is on par with that of other types of plans. One excellent resource for sizing up HMOs is the Washington, D.C.–based Consumers' Checkbook (202-347-9612). For a $12 fee, this nonprofit organization will send you customer ratings of hundreds of plans, along with a pamphlet on how to select the best one for your family.

CYBERTIP

Shopping for an HMO? Surfers on the World Wide Web can narrow their choices with a free on-line service called HMO SmartPages (http://www.buysmart.com/hmo). The service lets you access data on the dozens of individual HMOs available in each state. Among the things you'll learn: how many physicians and hospitals are affiliated with each; and whether or not a pediatrician can be assigned as the primary care doctor for your child.

IF YOU LACK HEALTH INSURANCE, GET COVERED

Maybe you're one of the 40 million Americans who have no health coverage whatsoever. The reason? You're floating from job to job and have avoided the obvious. Or, more likely, you think you simply can't afford it. Actually, you can't *not* afford this basic coverage—especially when you consider the financial devastation that a catastrophic illness or accident would bring. Cancer patients, for example, can easily rack up bills in the half-million-dollar range—that's far worse a sting than any medical premiums you pay today.

As previously explained, an HMO is generally the most affordable coverage. Regardless of the plan you choose, however, put a lock on costs by making sure the plan you select pays a maximum of no less than $500,000 in benefits for catastrophic coverage and carries a reasonable ceiling, or limit, on out-of-pocket expenses—generally no more than $2,500.

GET TO KNOW YOUR HEALTH PLAN FROM TOP TO BOTTOM

Quick: Does your health plan cover pregnancies? Answer: Probably, but with exceptions. Deliver the baby out of state and you just might leave the hospital with a baby *and* a big bill. How about nontraditional treatments, like chiropractic care? Think you're covered there? Chances are your plan allows some benefit. Where do you stand on cosmetic surgery, such as a nose job or breast augmentation? Those tune-ups will indeed cost you, since few plans cover "elective" or unnecessary procedures.

It may seem obvious, but you will save money on medical costs simply by picking through the nuts and bolts of your plan. You don't, for instance, want to wind up owing a huge hospital bill simply because you failed to get the preauthorization many insurers now require. It's wise to review the specifics of your health plan once every six months. What, exactly, are you covered for? How much are you required to pay out-of-pocket in any single year? Are dental checkups permitted once a year or every six months?

Two-career couples often have the luxury of choosing between two different insurance policies. Which one should you go with? In this instance, latch on to the plan that provides maximum benefits for your family's needs. This, by the way, may not be the costlier plan of the two, so don't base your decision on premium costs alone. Take the time you need to assess the benefits of each plan carefully. In fact, you'd both be wise to schedule an appointment with the company's benefits counselor to sort out the policies' fine points.

FILE CLAIMS PROMPTLY, AND BE A FANATIC ABOUT KEEPING RECORDS

Most health insurers will let you submit claims dated back one full year. Even the busiest sorts shouldn't let claims pile up for that long, though. By letting bills idle in a drawer, you allow your money to idle as well. Think about it: someone else is collecting interest on the payback you're entitled to.

Once you do get around to sending off those claims, keep copies of all bills and records for yourself, and guard them in a safe place for at least 12 months. When tax time rolls around, you'll hug yourself for having done so. With orderly records you can quickly determine whether you may write off your out-of-pocket health costs (they're deductible as long as they exceed 7.5% of your adjusted gross income). Glancing at your neat records toward year-end can help you plan further. You might even want to accelerate your January doctor's appointment into December, if the extra expense will help you hit the magic 7.5%.

There's another benefit to being organized. You can refer back to your records easily should a health claim be denied. Remember, if an insurer gives you the thumbs-down on a claim, you have every right to challenge the decision. In fact, one medical consumer group has found that nearly 80% of rejected Medicare claims are paid upon second try. To increase your chances for a favorable response, add a bit more information on your claim the second or third go-round.

SHOP AROUND FOR GOOD DOCTORS AND ASK FOR FEE RELIEF

If you lack insurance altogether, or if you are reimbursed only 50% for doctor visits, here's two words of advice: Comparison shop. Most patients aren't used to doing this, but with escalating doctor fees, you should. The broad constellation of doctor fees is also good reason to shop around for services. Remember, studies show that *fees for similar practitioners vary by more than 700%* in any given city. Your criteria for doctors, of course, should include more than price. For instance, one physician may represent more value than another by offering free "phone visits," taking the time to answer your questions and helping you to make informed treatment decisions about your care.

Once you find a doctor who makes you comfortable—by providing prompt service and clear answers to your medical queries—be sure to request an itemized bill of all charges. Review it with the doctor and ask if he or she would be willing to accept what your insurance pays. Depending on your out-of-pocket costs (say, 20% for a fee-for-service plan), you just may be able to cut a deal with some docs to lower those standard fees.

PASS ON OVERQUALIFIED DOCTORS FOR GENERAL NEEDS

Who wants to pay a cardiologist to combat the common cold? Believe it or not, many patients err by relying on one physician—often a specialist—no matter what their latest malady. While it is important to feel comfortable with your doctors, the price of familiarity may not always be worth it. Visiting a specialist such as a gynecologist for a simple matter like diarrhea simply doesn't make sense, as you're sure to pay twice as much as you would to see a general practitioner. Whenever a new medical problem arises, in fact, it's wisest to head to your primary care doctor first before seeing a specialist. He or she will probably grant you an appointment sooner than any specialist, and may even be able to give a quick diagnosis.

DON'T OVERPAY FOR DIAGNOSTIC TESTS

Unfortunately, some doctors may subject you to unnecessary or redundant medical tests, including MRIs, CAT scans, or EMGs. There are several reasons for this. Mainly, doctors face tremendous liability pressures and revert to so-called defensive medical practices. Their logic: By not exploring all possible symptoms and treatment avenues, they may expose themselves to lawsuits down the road. Also, more than a few physicians have a financial stake in the laboratories that perform diagnostic tests. To make sure you're not wasting precious dollars, ask your doctor to explain the need for costly tests, and request that he or she steer you to a facility that offers competitive rates.

If you're slated for a surgical procedure, save further by asking your doctor to schedule all necessary tests *before* you are admitted to the hospital. You'll pay less for the same tests on an outpatient basis, since hospitals must factor in overhead costs to patients already checked in. Once you are admitted, don't let the hospital staff repeat tests you've already taken.

SAVE 75% BY USING OUTPATIENT SERVICES

Maybe you like the idea of receiving flowers in the hospital. But who needs blooms when you could recover at home and save 25%–75% on your medical bills in the process? Dozens of medical procedures today can be performed safely on an *outpatient basis*, meaning the work is done in one day (at a hospital or clinic) without an overnight stay. It sure pays, then, to ask if your treatment can be handled this way. Take a gallbladder operation as an example. Stay in the hospital for three days (the average stay) and your bill upon checkout will be in the $9,000 range. The same procedure, done on an outpatient basis, would cost you less than half that sum, or about $2,000 to $3,000. Other common outpatient surgeries include vaginal hysterectomies and all cataract surgeries.

WATCH YOUR HOSPITAL BILLS FOR COSTLY ERRORS

These days the average hospital bill is a sickening $1,000 per day. Even if you have insurance that covers most of your costs (over 90%, typically), a stay of three to four days can leave you stuck with a substantial debt. As a preventative measure against mistakes and overcharges, then, smart medical consumers will keep their eyes peeled on the bill as it accrues.

Mistakes, you say? Yes, hospitals make them at a frightening rate. Audits find that fully 90% of all hospital bills have errors. Most of the time, the mistakes are in the hospital's favor. Errors aside, you may also get stung with downright unnecessary charges for tests your doctor didn't order. You stand to save hundreds of dollars, or even more, by ensuring that your bill is as accurate as possible. Here's how.

Keep a hospital journal. Writerly types may want to chronicle their stays for posterity; dollar pinchers will want to keep a written record for savings' sake. If you can't do it your-

112

self, have a relative post all tests, medications, and other items received (even those $15 slippers, which you can turn down altogether). Upon checkout, compare your notes with the itemized bill.

Request a bill that lists all charges. You want a printout that's itemized by individual charges, not merely by category. For example, your bill might list "Surgical Procedure, $4,500" or "Pharmacy, $800." This is not a full itemization. Insist on a bill that logs every pill, doctor charge, and room charge, by the day. Once in hand, scan this itemization for suspicious entries. Common errors include plain typos (where you're billed for 200 pills instead of 20); double entries (a charge that's erroneously repeated); and mystery charges (such as that appendectomy you never had).

Challenge mistakes. Your insurance company isn't likely to catch mistakes, so it is up to you to set the record straight. Alert your hospital's billing department to justify the charges against your own record and your patient chart. Following up in this way can yield a bigger payoff than you expected: to reward watchful eyes, some insurers actually let patients pocket any overcharges. If your query goes unsolved, or if you still dispute the bill, other avenues are worth pursuing. Alert your insurer to the discrepancy; or, for a fee of about $50–$100, hire a medical accounting firm to audit your bill. The largest firm is MedReview in Austin (800-397-5359).

SAVE 50%–70% ON PRESCRIPTION DRUGS AND VITAMINS

Many health policies today come bundled with automatic prescription drug savings—plans that let you stock up at the pharmacy for just $5 or $7 per prescription. If you don't have such a plan, try one of three remedies.

First, ask your physician to specify generic drugs on your prescriptions. These are the chemical equivalents of often costly name-brand drugs. For example, you could easily pay $85 for one hundred 60-milligram tablets of Cardizem, a widely prescribed heart medication. Its generic clone (diltiazem hydrochloride) would run you as little as $25 for the same order.

Even bigger savings can be found in your mailbox. Several mail-order pharmacies let you phone in orders, and discounts (even on name brands) run as high as 40%. Your doctor may be able to recommend a good mail-order company. Otherwise consider two of the largest: Action Pharmacy (800-452-1976) and Medi-Mail (800-922-3444). As an example, Medi-Mail charges about $16 for diltiazem hydrochloride, previously mentioned. Just be sure you can wait, since each takes about two weeks to deliver orders. If you still prefer to do your pharmacy shopping in person, compare prices. Depending on where you go, prices for the same prescription may vary by as much as 35%.

Americans also overpay on the *vitamin front,* where one of every three dollars spent goes wasted. In 1995 a special **MONEY** magazine investigation concluded that advertising hype and false medical claims are to blame for consumers' shelling out too much. Before you binge, ask your doctor for guidance; then shun high-priced brand names (Nature Made and Your Life) in favor of store brands. Believe it or not, store brands sold by Walgreen's, Rite-Aid, Wal-Mart, and Eckerd Drugs are identical to the fancy stuff but cost half as much.

SELECT DOCTORS WILLING TO ACCEPT MEDICARE AS FULL PAYMENT

Assuming you carry Medicare part B, do your best to locate doctors who take Medicare assignment as full payment. The program requires a 20% co-payment from patients. But after you've cleared your $100 deductible, ask your doc to take the government's 80% portion, called *assignment,* to satisfy the whole bill.

No matter which doctor you choose, it pays to be mindful that the law prohibits doctors from overcharging. Since any patient would be hard-pressed to calculate a doctor's fee vs. the legal maximum, here's another way to assess a bill for over-charges. The portion you owe should equal no more than 31% of the total fee; anything more probably means you're getting stung. If you have questions about doctor bills under Medicare, contact the New York City–based Medicare Rights Center at 212-869-3850 for free help and information.

"URGI-CARE" CENTERS SAVE 50% ON NONCRITICAL EMERGENCIES

Are you one of the millions of Americans who routinely use a hospital's emergency room for everyday health needs? Maybe you've decided that the annual flu virus doesn't require an $85 doctor's office visit? If so, so-called urgi-care centers (a round-the-clock doctor's clinic located in a strip mall near you) may fit the bill.

Nationwide, thousands of privately run clinics cater to patients with low-grade maladies. Naturally you wouldn't want to skimp on real emergencies. But for colds and broken bones, or even surgical procedures like cataract removal, urgent care centers are perfectly reliable. Cheaper than the typical office visit, such a center will charge 20%–50% less on nonemergency care. You'll find listings for these private clinics in your Yellow Pages, or for a referral to a center near you, phone the National Association for Ambulatory Care at 612-476-0015. (A tip: You'll do best with these centers by checking them out before you have a need for one. Look for doctors' credentials, cleanliness of facilities, and the crowd size in the waiting room.)

GET THE CHECKUPS YOU NEED

You know the saying "An ounce of prevention is worth a pound of cure." Most doctors would agree. Don't neglect the basic physical checkups recommended by the American Medical Association. For women over 18, these include an annual gynecological exam (with mammogram for those 50 and up). After age 40, men should be screened for prostate cancer each year. Taking care of your family in this way is sure to yield savings far more precious than the monetary kind.

INVEST IN A MEDICAL PRIMER

One way to lower health costs is to brush up on your medical smarts. Medical surveys routinely show that at least one in 10 doctor visits is unnecessary. This statistic isn't meant to make you ignore serious symptoms or ailments. But it does highlight the value of old-fashioned common sense. To help you size up basic health care situations (do you need to see a doctor for that itch, or is it just poison ivy?), grab a copy of the *Healthwise Handbook* ($16.95) or *Healthwise for Life* ($18.95). You can get both by calling Healthwise at 208-345-1161 or by checking your bookstore. The People's Medical Society also offers the excellent *Consumers Medical Desk Reference* in paperback (Hyperion; $19.95); it's a 760-page compendium of medical symptoms, treatments, and generic drug offerings.

GET A SECOND OPINION, AND THEN SOME

A second opinion, at its best, can be a lifesaver. It can also help avoid financial ruin, if you lack insurance and go in for an unnecessary $10,000 hysterectomy. *One in six medical diagnoses is reversed* upon second or third opinion. To protect themselves, most insurers require a second go-see before okaying surgery and other costly procedures. Even if yours doesn't, take the time to get the proper recommendations you need before agreeing to a costly or dangerous procedure.

PUSH YOUR HEALTH INSURER TO PAY FOR UNCOVERED BENEFITS

Believe it or not, some insurance companies will foot the bill for treatments not specified under your plan. Preventative measures like therapy and rehabilitation are worth negotiating, since they may eliminate the need for more costly remedies in the future. The argument is fairly straightforward: would your insurer rather ante up $200 or so per week *now* for psychotherapy treatments or fork over $3,000 a week *later* for a private psychiatric clinic? Speak with a supervisor at your health insurer to hammer out an arrangement that may save you both time and money.

THE BEST MEDICAL WEBSITES FOR CONSUMERS

In the old days, patients called on precious few resources—aside from the local library and newsstand publications—before going to see their doctors. The result: Medical consumers leaned on the reactive side, rarely challenging doctors and often agreeing to costly or unnecessary procedures. Today, powerful information available on the Web changes all that. Dozens of sites exist. Here are two of the best, as recommended by Charles Inlander of the People's Medical Society:

The U.S. National Library of Medicine's **Grateful Med** (http://igm.nlm.nih.gov/; $2.40 per hour usage fee) contains one of the largest publicly available databases on medical literature. By calling up recent articles from numerous medical

---

journals, you stand to be a sharply informed consumer even before you visit the doctor.

Healthworld (http://www.healthy.net) helps consumers boost their medical IQ with practical information on both mainstream and alternative practices. The site also has a bookstore where numerous medical publications are up for sale.

CHAPTER 7

How to Win Big in the College Sweepstakes

A college degree. That piece of parchment is as much a symbol of the American dream as a home with a two-car garage. Yet increasingly, for parents, the prospect of paying for just one college education is apt to trigger financial nightmares. Small wonder, as the average tuition for a private institution now tops $10,000 annually and is pushing $3,000 a year at public schools. With college prices increasing at a rate of 6.5% a year—or nearly twice the average annual rate of inflation—those figures aren't likely to ebb.

Perhaps you're already acquainted with some scary college cost scenarios. Parents cradling babes, for instance, can be sure that Junior's tuition will exceed the price of a 300-person wedding; the down payment on their home; and the cost of three cars—*three times over*. Put another way, to prepare for a three-year-old's public school education, parents would need to tuck away $300 per month. Procrastinate for just five years, and the punishment is severe indeed—the stakes nearly double, to a monthly burden of $577 a month. For most folks that's a monumental task, given other likely money woes, such as funding their retirement accounts and maybe even caring for an elderly parent.

Modest resources, however, shouldn't prevent your child from pursuing the education he or she deserves. Aggressive types have been able to tame their college bills by as much as 50%; and in this section we'll show you how. But first you may want to encourage Junior to take the term "four-year college" literally. Amazingly, 43% of all undergrads take five years to complete their bachelor's degree. Simply by finishing on time, your young Einstein can save the family well over $10,000.

Early Homework Pays Off Big

In the college sweepstakes—from admission, to scholarship aid, even dorm room dibs—timing counts. Your chances for getting a great college prize (acceptance into a terrific school *and* a financial package to match) will be much higher if you make some zealous moves as early as your child's sophomore year in high school.

Let's begin, then, with the touchy subject of grades. We can't stress enough that *the better you learn, the more you earn.* Well-rounded students who make the most of their secondary school years—enrolling (and excelling) in advanced science and math classes and pursuing one or two extracurricular activities—have the most money clout, period. Studious sorts who earn high marks both in class and on standardized tests such as the PSATs are in the running for one of 7,000 National Merit Scholarships worth anywhere from $1,000 to $40,000 plus. And, naturally, colleges earmark as much as 80% of their financial awards, or grants, to students with demonstrated academic prowess.

To get a head start on learning, and on saving, have your freshman or sophomore *earn college credits while still in high school.* By excelling in advanced placement (AP) classes, and/or taking college-level courses at a local community college, you stand to save handsomely. Dropping just one course from a student's roster can save about $700 at a public university. The credits, of course, are contingent upon the student's scoring well—generally a three or four out of a possible four on the AP exam, for instance. Because most private schools bill by the semester, not by the credit, this strategy works best at state schools and others that charge by the credit or course.

Bargain-conscious parents and students can hone their college choices if they take the time to *identify the most generous schools*. Some institutions, you'll discover, are downright Scrooges. Others are heavily endowed and will swing their vaults wide to lure the right candidates. Several publications, including **MONEY** magazine's annual college guide, cull listings of schools with the deepest pockets—or those who routinely give students the most merit-based aid as a percentage of total costs. For example, in the 1995 *College Guide,* we crowned Kentucky's Pikeville College as the most generous to its students. On average the school awards $6,386 annually per student, covering fully 71% of tuition, fees, and room and board. Princeton, on the other hand, has a far more paltry giving record. The university recently handed a skinny $3,997 to undergrads, covering just 14% of total costs. To gauge a school's generosity yourself, simply divide a college's own aid money by its enrollment. Both figures are easily obtained from the admissions or financial aid offices.

Of course, students can't rewrite their transcript history. One way to augment their eligibility for awards, however, is *by acing the dreaded Scholastic Assessment Test (SAT)*. Many academic scholarships have minimum SAT score strings attached, and sadly, some applicants find themselves out of the running by just 50 or 100 SAT points. For an investment of about $500, an SAT preparation course can help boost grades on a student's first or second stab at the exam. The $500 you pay could be one of your smartest investment moves ever, paying dividends to the tune of a $10,000 scholarship.

Another way to collect big bucks is to go after schools where your child's abilities will shine. Remember, talent magnets like Harvard and MIT make it tough for any applicant to stand out, much less get a handout. So be sure to investigate those schools where his or her test scores rank in the top five percentile of all entering freshmen.

Grades and test scores are vital stats, for sure. But don't overlook those institutions that are equally smitten with finely tuned skills in the arts, sports, and sciences. One example is Hartwick College in Oneonta, New York, which offers a lofty $6,000 to students with virtuosic musical talents. To help narrow your picks, check out the school's stats on entering freshmen and their complete lists of scholarship monies available through the school.

PINCHING TIP
When reviewing college choices, consider a school's total costs, not merely tuition and fees. You could bust your budget by forgetting about travel expenses, off-campus housing costs, and special tools (such as a computer).

Get Your Financial Aid Strategy in Place

Negotiate with a college? Absolutely. No matter what hand you're dealt in the financial aid game, most families can haggle for an even better package. According to the National Association of College and University Business Offices, plenty of small and private schools are willing to strike 30% off published tuition prices. If your kid has the right stuff—an enviable combination of great grades, high test scores, and the like—you may be able to lop *as much as 50% off* the school's asking price for tuition and room and board. Here's how.

MAKE AN EARLY SPLASH INTO THE FINANCIAL AID POOL

As easy as it is to watch those forms pile up on the dining room table, don't let inertia set in. Usually due on or before January 1, the standard federal Free Application for Federal Student Aid (FAFSA) determines how much, if any, financial assistance the government will award to your child. Both private and public schools use this standard form to dole out their own scholarship monies as well. Additionally, some schools now require the Financial Aid Profile for assessing the need for nongovernment dollars.

Getting your application in as early as possible won't assure you of a larger aid package. *The true dollar value of your award, however, could be affected dramatically by timing.*

Here's why. Working with a number of factors, a school will determine each family's financial "need." From there, financial aid officers will attempt to craft a package, often combining both *grants*, which don't have to be paid back, and *loans*, which must be repaid, usually with interest. Clearly the better deal is the free money.

Consider two applicants who each get award packages totaling $10,000. Early-bird Applicant A's package consists of $8,000 in grants and $2,000 in loans. Latecomer Applicant B may be just as needy, but his $10,000 package comprises $5,000 in grant money and $5,000 in loans. Bottom line: Even though each was "awarded" a $10,000 aid package, the true dollar value of Applicant A's package—depending on interest rates and repayment terms—could be worth thousands more than Applicant B's. So act early.

DON'T SETTLE FOR THE FIRST OFFER YOU GET

Say your child rips open one college's acceptance letter, and it contains a tempting financial aid package worth $10,000. An invitation from her first choice school follows, but with a promise of just $5,000 in aid. No need to sulk just yet. As they say at the tracks, let the races begin! Colleges today fully expect decisive students to appeal for more money. Negotiating is even key to their survival, since colleges must compete to attract the best candidates from a shrinking pool of college-bound seniors—a figure down roughly 14% since 1975.

To sweeten your deal, contact the financial aid office directly and ask them to reconsider. Remind them of your child's merits, and send along copies of other schools' acceptance letters. Be sure to flaunt more lucrative offers from other colleges—you may even care to fax copies to make your point. And don't forget to make a case about your family's overall need.

ANGLE TO KEEP MORE SCHOLARSHIP DOLLARS

As a rule, most schools will reduce their financial aid awards for every subsequent scholarship dollar students win. A bummer, for sure, but here's how to minimize the damage: Lobby the school to reduce the *loan* portion of its package and leave any grants in place. As we mentioned earlier, the grants-to-loan ratio will determine how much money you and/or your child will ultimately pay for a college degree.

LOCK IN YOUR AID PACKAGE—OR ELSE

Much like credit card issuers, colleges are big fans of so-called teaser rates. Benevolent U, for instance, may offer Junior a healthy $12,000 to walk through the freshman gates. Read that letter from the financial aid office more closely, however, and you may find that the deal expires after his first year. Yes, it smacks of cheating, but this bait-and-switch technique is fairly routine at many institutions. To protect your position, get a guarantee in writing from the school that its money deal is good for *all four years.*

WATCH FOR ERRORS

Though not common, it is possible for a college to use incorrect data when calculating an aid package. If you receive wildly different offers from equally rich schools, you might ask that the financial aid office double-check the information used (such as you and your spouse's salary and the number of your dependents). As an example, an incorrect salary, spiked accidentally by $10,000, could result in a loan package worth thousands less than you deserve.

PINCHING TIP

If your application for financial aid gets denied for freshman year, don't give up. Keep in touch with the financial aid office and let them know of any circumstances (such as having an additional child in school) that might make you eligible for aid in subsequent years.

Harvard or Bust:
Getting the Lowest-Cost Loans

Don't be so quick to sap your family's resources to pay for your child's campus experience. Financial planners agree that the call of higher education shouldn't override other long-term goals, especially your own retirement.

For most families, then, borrowing at least some college money is the reality. Where should you turn? While your 401(k) plan may be a ready source for cash, think twice before you fleece it. Such loans must be repaid in full, plus interest, within five years. Fail to do so and you'll get slapped with harsh penalties and taxes that can easily exceed half of the amount owed.

No matter what type of loan you choose, remember that *the longer the term, the more you'll pay in interest.* So after the tassel's been turned at commencement, choose the most abbreviated payment schedule you or your young scholar can afford. Among the low-cost options for both parents and students:

Stafford loans. Subsidized by the federal government and available to students who show need, Staffords let scholars borrow anywhere from $2,700 to $8,500 each school year, at a modest interest rate of about 8.50% (plus a 4% loan origination fee). Uncle Sam graciously pays the interest tab on these loans as long as your child is matriculated in school; upon graduation, repayment terms span anywhere from 10 to 30 years. (Again, the shorter the term, the less you'll pay in interest.) Less needy students can usually qualify for unsubsidized Staffords, but there the interest meter starts ticking during school, unlike the situation with their subsidized counterparts. You can pick up an application for Stafford loans at most financial aid offices or apply directly with a private lender (call the Federal Student Aid Information Center at 800-433-3243 for more information).

PLUS loans. The government also extends a helping hand to Mom and Dad, through its Parent Loan to Undergraduate Students (PLUS) program. As its acronym suggests, a PLUS loan is meant to bridge any gap between a student's total college costs and financial aid. Available to most parents with good credit, PLUS loans have a 10-year term and offer favorable rates that fluctuate with Treasury bill rates. As a rule, figure on paying several percentage points below a bank's personal loan or home-equity loan offerings. You can apply for a PLUS loan either at private lenders or, in some cases, directly through the college.

PINCHING TIP
Students can save thousands on their Stafford loans by having them bought by Sallie Mae (that's the federally chartered Student Loan Marketing Association) after 48 timely payments. On a four-year, $20,000 loan at 8.25%, borrowers stand to save $1,156 over a 10-year repayment term. Call Sallie Mae at 800-891-4599 and ask for more information on its Great Rewards program.

Home-equity loans. Most homeowners can harness up to 80% of the equity in their homes, taking out sums as needed with a home-equity line of credit. More flexible than a straight home-equity loan, this allows you to draw on a predetermined credit line as needed. The interest on such loans up to $100,000 is fully tax-deductible, but the standard warning for these types of loans still applies: if you get clumsy in making payments, you risk losing your home.

Borrow against your cash value life insurance policy. Lots of insurance salespeople hype cash value insurance (also called whole life, variable life, or universal life insurance) as a great way to finance a college education. While visions of Harvard should never drive you to purchase such a policy (see Chapter 8), this variety does offer some relief. Most allow you to borrow the full cash value of your policy, usually at a favorable rate (recently about 7%). So assuming you saw fit to buy one of these policies, this option is worth considering. One hitch: Should you die before full repayment of the loan, the entire balance, plus interest, will be deducted from your death benefit.

Finding Scholarship Gold

Sure, most of the nation's schools—86%, to be precise—offer various types of scholarship dollars. How much your child catches may hinge on a host of criteria, such as his or her academic "merit," your financial "need," and in some cases, racial or ethnic background. It's not an autopilot process, however. Depending on the school, or the prize, you may have to apply separately for a specific grant. Other awards take all applicants into consideration. The single most comprehensive guide to these scholarships is *The As and Bs of Academic Scholarships* (Octamaron press; $7), which lists over 100,000 no-need, or merit-based, awards at 1,200 schools.

Don't dare stop there. Some of the greatest scholarships available today—worth some $1.25 billion—are doled out by private sources. Most parents and students have heard of the Olympic-size awards. A few examples: Coca-Cola gifts up to $20,000 to students working for community causes; Westinghouse bestows as much as $40,000 on science whizzes; and Tylenol hands out scholarships worth $10,000 for overall academic excellence.

Realistically, most students will have to do some serious pole-vaulting to land these bucks. The good news in all this is that the spoils aren't for geniuses only. Sure, top grades and sharp talents—such as music and science proficiency—give many students an edge. But so too can oddball abilities and affiliations. For instance:

- Superpatriots who eloquently voice their allegiance via audio essay can qualify for grants of $1,000 to $20,000 from the Voice of Democracy Program, administered by the Veterans of Foreign Wars (816-968-1117).

128

• For those students whose parents have any remote connection to harness racing (say, as a breeder, trainer, or stable keeper), five prizes of $3,000 each await from the Harness Tracks of America (602-529-2525).

As you can see, then, perseverance is what you'll need to find treasures worth thousands. And on that score, a word of caution. Many so-called college scholarship search services, including dozens on the Internet, will be happy to take your money and do the sleuthing for you. Fact is, most of these outfits do little more, or less, than you could on your own. Others are outright scams. Save the $200 or so they charge and conduct your own diligent search:

Head to the guidance counselor's office for leads. Your child's guidance counselor should have a trove of information on local scholarships and may know about unusual scholarships bestowed on former students. Also take the time to browse through any scholarship books in the guidance office.

Look for gold in your backyard. Many of the private scholarship dollars up for grabs, believe it or not, lurk very close to home. Fully 90% of all companies that employ 1,000 or more make college scholarship awards. In addition, your church, social club, local newspaper, fraternal groups—all are likely to offer scholarships to college-bound seniors. Be sure to check both those organizations in your own community, as well as others in the city where your child plans to attend college.

Hit the stacks. Among the very best reference books listing thousands of scholarship possibilities are these:

Winning Scholarships for College: An Insider's Guide (Henry Holt; $10.95). Marriane Ragins, the author of this book, really knows her stuff. A few years ago she attracted more scholarship money than she could use—$400,000, to be exact.

Another 1,700 scholarship opportunities are explored in *Fund Your Way through College* (Visible Ink Press; $19.95), famous for its paperback listing of 100,000 no-need (merit-based) scholarships.

For a regional tour of grant monies available, check out *College Scholarships and Financial Aid* (Arco; $21.95).

Learn to recognize the fakes. Be alert to the fact that not every "scholarship offer" is legit—not even the ones that sound aboveboard, using "Federal" or "National" in their titles. Use your good judgment when applying. If it sounds too good to be true (promising guaranteed winnings, declaring that everyone is eligible, etc.), it probably is. Be particularly suspicious of any unsolicitied offerings and any outfit that demands an application fee of any kind. Legitimate scholarship sources don't beg.

PINCHING TIP

The adage "There's folly in delay" applies to the tenth power with college scholarships. To increase your child's chances of winning a coveted prize, have him or her start tracking down scholarships earlier rather than later. The hunt should begin no later than sophomore year.

CYBERTIP

An A+ scholarship source on the Net is fastWeb (http://www.studentservices.com/fastweb). This service asks for specific student information and tries to match applicants with legitimate scholarship sources. You'll also find numerous calculators to help you project financial aid needs and student loan costs.

Four Ways to Graduate Richer and Quicker

TRANSFER FOR DOLLARS

Harvard, Yale. Competitive? Yes. Costlier than a Lamborghini? You bet. Except, that is, for students able to rack up cheap first- and second-year credits elsewhere, then trade their transcripts for Ivy at the final stretch. The idea is simple enough. Have your child enroll in a state or community college for the first year or two. At sophomore or junior year, have them put in a transfer application to the school of their dreams. This tactic, which can shave $20,000 or more off of a degree, is an especially good one for students who need to put punch in their grades. Before applying to a more prestigious and expensive school, however, make sure you understand exactly how many credits are applicable to the new degree.

SAVE UP TO 25% ON A THREE-YEAR PLAN

If your student is the Doogie Howser type, he or she may be able to marathon through four years' worth of classics and chem labs in just three years. Today, roughly 200 colleges and universities advertise and encourage such rapid degrees.

Granted, the quickie BA isn't for everyone, especially given how 43% of all students take five years to complete their studies. Another drawback is a short-changed campus life. But for those students who can hang tough, tuition savings are substantial—as much as $20,000 at schools like Albertus Magnus College in Connecticut or Middlebury College in Vermont. To find out if an institution offers three-year degree completion, contact the school admissions office directly.

BATTLE THE BULGE WITH A TUITION CAP

No, we aren't mixing metaphors here about the infamous freshman 15 and the graduating senior's mortarboard. Rather, we're suggesting you fight ballooning tuition rates with something called a *price guarantee*. Having routinely outpaced inflation rates by two percentage points each year, a small band of competition-savvy colleges are putting a lid on costs. At Michigan State and Rice Universities, for instance, arriving freshmen are guaranteed that tuition hikes won't exceed the consumer price index, or about 3.2% annually. Ask any colleges you're courting if they have such a policy. At the very least, some colleges will agree to waive tuition for a fifth year, should the extended stay be due to oversubscribed classes during senior year.

COMBINE GRADUATE STUDIES WITH THE FOUR-YEAR DEGREE

Even before they get their first syllabus, many freshman students have set on a master's degree in a field such as law or business. Or, once they assimilate into college life, a school's continuing education options may look more and more attractive.

Have your child check out one of the 350 schools that offer five-year master's programs (common degrees: masters of arts, journalism, even business). By enrolling in one, he or she may get graduate credentials in half the usual time. Many schools will admit students to these programs when they apply as freshmen; others give preferential treatment to matriculated undergrads. Aside from saving thousands on tuition, the five-year route also spares the time and cost of applying to grad school separately.

WHY "TUITION PREPAYMENT" PLANS DON'T ALWAYS SAVE YOU MONEY

A growing number of colleges are offering so-called tuition prepayment plans. Many people assume that these plans are designed to save them money. However, that's not always the case.

One such option is really a college investment plan, allowing parents to prepay tuition as far as 10 years in advance of their child's freshman year. The amount paid, in monthly installments, is based on today's tuition rates, sparing parents those costly 6.5%-a-year tuition hikes. (So far, Alabama, Alaska, Florida, Massachusetts, Ohio, Pennsylvania, and Texas offer such programs.) By starting early enough, you could easily satisfy your kid's college bill before he or she is out of high school.

Of course, there's a downside. And it may cost you big time. Your child will be limited to the public school system in your state and must still satisfy regular admissions criteria. Should he or she face rejection, or decide to attend school elsewhere, you will likely get back only the money you put in, with no interest. For parents who've contributed over a 10-year period, that could amount to a loss of several thousands of dollars.

CHAPTER 8

Lower All Your Insurance Costs

Got a new home to protect? Dependents to care for? A specific event—like a wedding—to cover? Has the financial world got a magic word for you: insurance. Modern times, it seems, have demanded all sorts of products from the insurance industry. In the face of incredible competition, insurers today will happily sell any policy for whatever ails you: a personal liability policy to guard against litigious types (for when your boss slips and falls in your living room); insurance to cover your cruise (should it be canceled); and for the truly risk-averse, even a policy to cover your hamster's braces. No kidding.

Comforting stuff for sure, but such peace of mind, of course, costs—in many cases *too much*. Just consider: The average American family spends 6% of its household income on insurance. According to the National Insurance Consumer Organization, at least 10% of all premium dollars are wasted on needless coverage. Of course, all this adds up to a fine deal for insurance salespeople, whose rapturous pitches often result in huge commissions. So while insurance for most of us is a necessity, it's imperative that you pick and choose—and understand—

your policies carefully. You want to be neither overinsured (buying costly, useless, or redundant coverage) nor underinsured.

After a careful appraisal of your individual needs, use this chapter to *save as much as $500 a year on insurance premiums*. But first, consider some universal tips on cutting all types of insurance expenses.

COMPARISON SHOP

Go ahead, kick the tires of an insurance policy just as you would a new car. When shopping for any major policy, start by checking the rates of at least a half dozen carriers. Don't be surprised if you get quotes that are as much as $100 apart for identical coverage. As your beacon, consider the following low-cost carriers first: State Farm (for homeowners); Amica (auto); and Northwestern (disability). You can find them in your White Pages business directory, or dial 800-242-6422 for a phone rep at Amica.

PICK A SOLID INSURER

History shows us that an insurance policy is only as sound as the company that backs it. Just consider the 80 insurance companies whose assets were seized by state regulators over the past six years, not to mention numerous others forced to file for bankruptcy protection. For that reason, you want to do business with fiscally fit firms scoring top grades (in other words, the ones best able to pay all claims) from nationally recognized rating services. The five to consult are: A. M Best (908-439-2200); Standard & Poor's (212-208-1527); Duff & Phelps (312-368-3157); Moody Investor's Service (212-553-0377); and Weiss Research (800-289-9222).

RAISE YOUR DEDUCTIBLES

A sure way to reduce premiums on just about any type of insurance is to raise the deductible (that's the amount you are responsible for paying out-of-pocket before benefits kick in). By augmenting the deductible on your homeowners insurance from $250 to $1,000, for example, you'd save about 20% each year on your policy. This same rule will yield substantial savings with auto and health insurance, too.

GET THE DISCOUNTS YOU DESERVE

The insurance industry reserves many types of discounts for specific customers or groups. These rebates span from the wide ranging to the superspecific. For instance, good students probably qualify for special discounts on auto premiums. And members of Boston's St. Augustine Parish rate a 10% discount on Plymouth Rock Assurance's auto policies. It always pays, then, to inquire about special breaks available to you. Keep in mind that some policies, such as homeowners and auto insurance, have numerous coverages (for things like theft and liability and collision). So before you pay up, be sure to find out whether rebates will be applied to all or part of the policy.

SEEK GROUP COVERAGE

Like any other business, buying in bulk in the insurance world pays off. That's why group rates can be as much as 50% below what an individual would pay. Professional groups, churches, fraternal organizations, alumni associations, and other outfits, such as the American Association of Retired Persons (AARP), may be a source of relief. Two examples: The American Anthropological Association (703-528-1902) accepts anyone for membership and offers health coverage for less than $400 a month for couples. Another group, the Chicago-based Parents without Partners, lets single parents join for $40 a year and offers discounted health coverage to its members.

THINK TWICE BEFORE FILING MINOR CLAIMS

Yes, you pay those premiums for a reason. So when your car gets scratched in a parking lot, or when your living room window shatters during a thunderstorm, you should race to file a claim, right? Not so fast. As it turns out, insurance companies aren't thrilled about writing checks, and they often show their displeasure by spiking premiums. Even after you have satisfied the deductible on a policy, try to file only major claims you can't afford to pay out-of-pocket. (The exception: any type of auto accident involving another driver. For liability purposes, you should always report such incidents.)

PINCHING TIP

Free information on insurance rates may be available from your state's insurance department. Such consumer guides are published by about half of the states and provide comparative data on all the insurance companies who write policies there. To locate your state insurance department, check the government pages in your phone book.

Put a Dent in Your Auto Insurance Premiums

We'll be blunt here: it isn't cheap to protect your driving machine against collision, theft, and liability. Due in part to rampant lawsuits, plus high medical and car repair costs, auto premium rates tend to surge by roughly 8% annually—or nearly twice as high as most other consumer prices. In 1981 the typical premium was a scant $290 per year. These days that figure is a musclebound $800. First-time car owners and young adults get rear-ended the worst, with premiums for a 20-year-old single male costing about 50% more than coverage for an older driver. Another reason to be alert when shopping for coverage: Within the same city, identical auto policies can vary in price by hundreds of dollars.

Because your car's model will affect your premiums, it pays to *take auto insurance rates into account before you buy.* Certain low-risk cars—those with below average claims rates—can spare you several hundred dollars a year in premiums. An example: The $11,000 Honda Civic is generally a "high" insurance cost car, while the $21,000 Buick Regal is considered a "low" insurance cost set of wheels.

Put a break on your own costs by first figuring out how *much insurance you need and no more.* For example, most insurance packages bundle coverage for bodily injury liability, collision, uninsured motorist coverage, and property-damage liability. Review your other insurance policies to see if any provide duplicate coverage. Other tips:

CHECK RATES WITH INDEPENDENT AND OTHER AGENTS

Independent agents peddle policies from several different insurers and can sometimes get you top-of-the-line rates. (If their quotes run a bit high, fat commissions are probably to blame.) In any case, you'll want to compare their rates with those of competitors who rely less heavily on commissions. Try companies that employ their own sales teams (such as State Farm and Nationwide) or insurers who sell policies directly to the public via toll-free numbers (such as Amica at 800-242-6422 and USAA at 800-531-8080).

GET A BREAK WHEN INSURING YOUR COLLEGE-BOUND KID

Assuming they drive around campus infrequently, students attending school more than 100 miles from home can qualify as "occasional operators" on Mom and Dad's policy. Typical savings: about $350 per year less than what you'd pay to insure them separately.

GO BACK TO DRIVING SCHOOL

A brief road course costing about $50 could be well worth the investment, yielding discounts of 5% to 10% off many insurers' collision rates. Drivers over the age of 55 stand to get the biggest breaks here.

STOP SPEEDING, AND DRIVE SAFELY

A simple thing like a clean driving record (avoiding traffic tickets and wrecks) can save you as much as 10% within a three-year period. Keep driving problem free for three more years, and most companies will grant you 15% off.

NIX COLLISIONS COVERAGE ALTOGETHER ON OLD MODELS

Any vehicle worth less than $1,000 (that '76 Toyota idling in the driveway?) isn't worth insuring to the hilt. If you don't know the current value of your old wheels, take a look at the used-car guides available at your local library.

CHECK OUT YOUR OPTIONS

If your car is "loaded" with factory or dealer options, some of those extras can rate you a discount, too. Among them, antilock brakes, air bags, and car alarms can all help reduce the cost of your premiums 5%–10%.

PINCHING TIP

Shopping for a car? A free booklet, *Injury, Collision & Theft,* is available from the Insurance Institute for Highway Safety. It gives a model-by-model breakdown of car safety records—statistical information that can steer you to a low-insurance car. Write to Publications, P.O. Box 1420, Arlington, Va. 22210.

Homeowners and Renters Insurance Savings

Each year Americans fork over $20 billion to protect their homes. Think of homeowners insurance—which covers both property and liability—as a three-pronged safety net, designed to cover your house, your belongings, and your family, should you get sued for on-site accidents. Finding generous savings here can be somewhat tricky, since most insurers set rates based on your home's location, age, and estimated rebuilding costs. (As a starting point, however, it may help to know that the average home dweller paid between $400 and $1,000 to insure a $150,000 house. Apartment renters paid $100–$300 on average.) There are plenty of ways for you to trim costs, however.

SHED YOUR OLD RIDERS AND FLOATERS

Perhaps you purchased a rider for Uncle Emmet's $5,000 violin years ago but have since given it to your Paganini-inspired niece. Or you insured that $7,000 mink coat, bought back in the fat '80s, but have since sided with the antifur movement. You'll want to make sure you've canceled such coverage and that your insurer is no longer charging you.

BE A SAFETY BUG

Many insurers will cut a 10% discount to homeowners who own alarm systems routed directly to their police and fire stations. That's a nifty reduction for those who already have such a device. Otherwise think twice about installing one just to snare an insurance discount. The savings may not warrant it.

SAVE BY PAYING MORE

Although they cost more than other policies, *guaranteed replacement* coverage can save the day should a disaster befall your castle. For roughly 15% more than other policies (most pay only 80% of rebuilding costs), such a contract ensures that you'll get the full amount necessary to reconstruct your home from scratch. One caveat: Because these premium rates tend to rise with inflation, review your adjustments annually.

INSURE YOUR HOME AND CARS WITH THE SAME COMPANY

Insurers will love you for giving them more business. Sure, they're happy to insure your home, but they'll swoon when you toss your cars into the equation. You'll smile, too, since consolidating coverage this way can reduce premiums by as much as 30%. As an extra perk, keeping your cars and home under one insurance roof lets you buy excess liability coverage for both. You probably already have liability insurance for your home and car—it protects you in the event that you cause harm to others due to negligence. Most policies pay only up to $500,000, but an *umbrella liability policy* covers larger losses. This coverage is cheap: typically about $100 to $250 per year for up to $1 million worth of extra protection.

CHOOSE A NEWER HOME, IF POSSIBLE

The insurance industry gives preferential treatment to modern homes, as they tend to be easier to maintain and rebuild than, say, a turn-of-the-century Victorian. Brand-new homes get the most favor. Expect to save about 5% to 20% for homes that were erected within the past five years.

143

PINCHING TIP

Drop that *@#*$% PMI insurance! If your lender required you to take out private mortgage insurance on your home loan, try to get rid of it the moment you accrue 20% equity in your home. Many lenders will cancel this obligation—if you ask—for a potential savings of hundreds of dollars each year on your mortgage.

Save on Health and Disability

With medical costs going through the roof, everybody is grasping for ways to tame costs. Gone are the days when your employer picked up the insurance tab—most now require workers to contribute at least a few dollars from each paycheck. And for the 40 million Americans who are not covered by such a plan, savings are even more crucial. Chapter 6 discusses many ways to save on your overall health costs, including some insurance angles. The following tips are worth considering, too.

CONSIDER MANAGED CARE OPTIONS TO SAVE 80%

At roughly half of all U.S. companies, comprehensive insurance policies have been supplanted by so-called managed care options. Called health maintenance organizations (HMOs) or preferred provider organizations (PPOs), these types of plans control costs by limiting your choice of medical providers. HMOs, for instance, restrict you to a list of "in-network" doctors. Typical cost: $100 per month for a family of four, with no deductibles. (For more information on these plans, see Chapter 6.)

SPOUSES: SELECT THE BETTER PLAN

If both you and your spouse have access to an employer's health plan, review each one carefully to see which provides the more comprehensive coverage at the lower cost. Valuable benefits to watch for include dental care, annual physical exams, and prescriptive eyewear.

SAVE ON DISABILITY INSURANCE

Should you become ill or injured, and unable to perform your job, you'll surely need disability insurance. Employers often provide some type of disability coverage, but it may replace only 50% or less of your regular wages. You may want to purchase a policy that protects you more fully, for up to 80% of your total income. Unfortunately, your search for rates will yield searing results. The best way to save is to *go for the longest waiting period.* Most plans start paying benefits about 30 days after you become disabled. By stretching that period out to, say, 90 days, you stand to cut your premiums by as much as 25%.

CYBERTIP

Shopping for an HMO? Surfers on the World Wide Web can narrow their choices with a free on-line service called HMO SmartPages (http://www.buysmart.com/hmo). The service lets you access data on the dozens of individual HMOs available in each state. Among the things you'll learn: how many physicians and hospitals are affiliated with each; and whether or not a pediatrician can be assigned as the primary care doctor for your child.

Slash Your Life Insurance Costs

Beware overzealous life insurance sellers. Read that again if you are young with no dependents. Why? Because much of what's sold as "life insurance" is hawked as an "investment product." By knowing the difference—and sizing up your risks—you can save wads of cash.

The life insurance product most likely to be disguised as an "investment" is cash value insurance. Unlike straightforward term insurance, which pays only when you die, cash value policies (also called whole, variable, or universal life) buy you two things: life insurance and a tax-deferred savings account. Your premium dollars fund both, and the savings account—which builds up a "cash value" over time—earns a guaranteed interest rate.

In some cases (usually for wealthy or conservative types who require low-risk, tax-advantaged investments) cash value life insurance can make sense. But unless you insure for the long haul, you'll surely lose. By keeping such a contract for less than 10 years, you'd likely forfeit most of your cash value to fees and commissions. No wonder financial planners agree that most of us are better off buying stocks, bonds, and other investments to build for the future. Life insurance is best kept a separate matter.

That said, plain old-fashioned term insurance is the purest form of life insurance and by far the cheapest. A 40-year-old nonsmoking male might expect to pay $325 a year for $300,000 worth of term insurance. That's about 60% less than he'd fork over for the same amount of cash value insurance. Of course, those premiums will rise with age. But when comparing term rates, don't be swayed by the lowest quotes you get. Ask an agent to project rates for five, 10, and even 20 years down the road. You may find that the term policy with the lowest initial rate isn't the long-term winner.

Other tips to enrich your survivors:

QUIT SMOKING AND STAY TRIM

Smokers who quit the habit can often halve their life insurance costs. A hefty discount is also available to overweight persons who manage to attain the average recommended weight for their size.

DON'T BUY IT UNLESS YOU NEED IT

Life insurance salesfolk would be happy to swathe young unmarried types in a $100-per-month insurance policy. Trouble is, they probably don't need it. The purpose of insurance is not to start an investment cache—by all means purchase mutual funds and stocks for that. Instead, use life insurance as a way to replace a family member's income in the event of his or her demise. Worry about this type of coverage only if you have dependents or sizable assets. Then plan on securing coverage that's worth six to eight times your gross annual income. When figuring your needs, don't forget the coverage offered by your job. Most large companies provide nominal life insurance (equal to one or two years' salary) as a standard benefit.

BE ON THE LOOKOUT FOR LOW-LOADS

Not a reference to the weight issue just mentioned, a low-load policy simply signals smaller commissions and, hence, lower commissions. Most low-load insurers, such as USAA and Ameritas, charge between 10% and 20% in sales commissions on your first-year premiums—that's about half of what other agents take. You can get hassle-free price quotes from three sources: Quotesmith (800-556-9393); Term Quote (800-444-8376); and SelectQuote (800-608-7754).

Insurance Policies You (Probably) Just Don't Need

The insurance industry busily spins out new policies to prey on your every fear: Maybe your wedding will get canceled. Perhaps you'll get trounced by bulls in Spain—before that stereo is paid off. Again, covering such risks may provide comfort to a few. But your chances of encountering any of the scenarios described below are minuscule. One of the best ways to lower your insurance costs, in fact, is to pass on bogus coverage you simply do not need. Among the policies to avoid:

Credit life insurance. Maybe you're taking out a car loan or charging a high-end home entertainment system at a big store. You've barely completed the transaction when the ugly possibility gets raised: What if you were to die before you paid off the debt? That's the ominous sell line for credit life insurance, which for as much as $300 promises to cover your loan payments if you make an early exit. Be grateful that someone, er, *cares* about you—but decline this policy anyway. Rather than pay monthly premiums of as much as $20 on a four-year auto loan, set up a rainy-day savings account to cover catastrophes. Or, for debts that exceed $10,000, consider adjusting your life insurance coverage.

Home warranties. Your real estate agent, or the developer of your home, may offer you a warranty of sorts that promises to protect your palace against major repairs and defects. They'll cost about $300 to $550 and are hardly worth the price. New houses generally require no insurance beyond the standard homeowners policy. Even for older homes, "warranties" present a grave risk: the insurance is only as sound as its seller. Should your agent or developer go belly up—as more than 14,000 have since 1988—you run the risk of holding a useless warranty.

Travel insurance. Are you a nervous flier with visions of your plane going down in flames? Concerned that a last-minute emergency will prevent you from hopping aboard the *Love Boat?* Such fears may be valid, but travel insurance is the wrong way to treat them. Travel policies, which may bundle coverage for trip cancellation, baggage loss, and flight catastrophes, are costly and riddled with exclusions. (For instance, you might pay $30 for a trip cancellation policy that will reimburse you only up to $350.) Also, most are secondary policies, meaning they pay up only in the event your primary coverages—such as home and medical—won't.

Cancer insurance. This dubious coverage costs about $300 a year and promises to cover you should the cancer roulette wheel point your way. Most policies pay between $75 and $100 for each day you're laid up in the hospital. Of course, this won't make a dent in the average $800-a-day hospital stay. And as we just stressed, this coverage is often redundant against any major medical policies.

Wedding insurance. Now, if such insurance covered you against cold feet—getting left at the altar, so to speak—it might be worth it. Instead, it covers you for prepaid expenses (such as the catering hall) in the event of last-minute cancellations. You should pass on this coverage, which costs anywhere from $100 to $600 plus. In any case, you may already be protected by your catering/wedding facility's policy or your homeowners policy.

CHAPTER 9

Save Big on "Big-Ticket" Items

Plus, When It Actually Pays to Pay More

Trust us, bigger isn't necessarily better. For consumers, that maxim applies whether an item swells in either size *or* price. Judging by today's retailing scene, though, you'd be hard-pressed to convince Americans that small is beautiful. Witness the demand for big-screen television sets (sales are up threefold since 1992) or the rage for *über*-wheels like the Ford Explorer (dealers have long waiting lists). Then consider our knack for piling up big debts to acquire such stuff. In 1996 consumers carried more than $444 billion worth of debt on credit cards alone. You can bet that much of that red ink flowed to finance big purchases such as camcorders, furs, and jewels—the sorts of items that are too costly to cover in one pay period but are affordable enough to slide in under your credit limit. As this chapter will show you, however, buying a "big-ticket" item doesn't have to turn you into a big spender. Especially if you keep the following in mind.

THINK ABOUT RENTING INSTEAD OF BUYING

Happily, hungry consumers of all types are finding a midpoint between owning and doing without. Rather than say "Charge it," their motto has become "Rent it." You, too, may find that it makes more sense to lease a budget-busting item—especially if it's likely to get only limited use. Haven't checked out the rental items up for grabs lately? (Maybe that floor waxer at the grocery store was the last thing you took on loan.) Then you'll surely be surprised by the zany array of stuff that can be yours for the night or for the month.

Consider the possibilities, starting with a jazzy museum print featured in the Seattle Art Museum. At $1,500 it hurts your wallet. Try renting and you can hang it in your living room for three months (long enough to impress those visiting in-laws) for as little as $100. Or maybe you worry that an exercise bike may tote up more dust than miles. You just might consider renting that, too—perhaps until those extra five pounds melt away. Fancy yourself in a couture gown, but can't afford the designer's $1,000 price tag? You'll be queen for a day by renting the same frock. The list goes on, from sailboats to jukeboxes, even animals. See for yourself by looking in the Yellow Pages under "Rental Services." There you're sure to find dozens of categories. Or for more information on rental thrills in your area, contact the American Rental Association at 800-334-2177. (And see the box "10 Cool Things You Can Rent.")

TEN COOL THINGS YOU CAN RENT

- Pianos ($35 for monthly tunes vs. $2,700 to buy)
- Hot Tubs ($80 for a month-long soak vs. $3,000 for unlimited dunks)
- Slot Machines ($60 for a weekly thrill vs. $2,000 to buy)
- Wedding Dresses ($250 for the big day vs. $1,500 to sit in your attic for decades)
- Museum Prints ($100 to impress the in-laws for a month vs. $1,000 to own)
- Stair Steppers ($50 a month to sweat vs. $1,200 to buy)
- Robots ($50 to star in your next party vs. $1,000 to own)
- Gazebos ($70 to shelter the bride vs. $2,500 to build)
- Snow Blowers ($20 for a week of easy snow removal vs. $800 to own)
- Karaoke Machines ($40 for one night of embarrassment vs. $1,800 to drive your friends away forever)

DON'T BINGE ON BIG-TICKET ITEMS WITH PLASTIC

Cruising the electronics aisles with a credit limit of $5,000 or more, many of us experience a false sense of wealth. Sure, you can plunk down the plastic and pay it off whenever. But unless you have a plan—say, to clear the debt in a month or so—charging big-ticket items can leave you stuck with a gruesome interest bill. Take that $1,000 camcorder as an example. By charging it on a card with an 18% annual percentage rate (the nation's average APR), and paying only the minimum amount due each month, it would take an astounding 12 years to retire the debt. Along the way you'd get nicked for *$979 in interest charges alone.*

LEARN TO BE AN ACE NEGOTIATOR

Go ahead, jump in the ring. These days haggling over prices is required if you're spending over $500 on an item. In fact, most shopkeepers expect it. Skilled negotiators can lop 20% or better off prices if they know how to play by the rules.

Keep your cool and use flattery. Walking away with the right price is all about attitude. Don't act as if you must have a particular TV or fur—that's a tip-off that you'll pay any price. Never be rude or obnoxious, since most salesfolk would rather tank a sale than appease demanding types. Instead try a little flattery, and flash a smile. You might say, "Gee, I really love shopping here, but I could sure use a break on this price." Or, "Hi, Bob, remember me? You were so helpful when I bought that TV two months ago, and I'd love for you to help me with another purchase today."

Always have a target price. Rather than waffle on price, let a seller know, up front, how much you are willing to pay for an item. A shopkeeper or store manager is apt to take you more seriously if you stick to your guns. If they don't like the deal, they'll spare your time by cutting off negotiations earlier rather than later.

Know an item's cost. How much should the object of your desires really cost? You can get a feel for the "right" asking price by knowing an item's markup (that's the difference between a seller's wholesale cost and their asking, or retail, price). Clothing, for instance, carries an ugly markup of 50%–100%. Large appliances generally have a 15% markup, and cars carry markups of roughly 5%–10%. If you're in the dark about the real price, use this rule: Offer 15% less than the asking price.

Know the market. Is business bland or brisk at the store where you're shopping? What about at competitors down the street? Are certain model cars flying off the lots, leaving the dealer a bloated inventory of white convertibles (just the car you want!)? Finding the gaps in a storekeeper's business can lead you to the bargains. The lower the demand for a product, the better your chance to offset the price.

Ask to deal with the manager. Even if the store has a strict "no discounts" policy, a manager may be able to bend the rules a bit by giving you some sort of concession, like a $50 store credit, an extra shirt, or a few free videotapes.

Spend quality time in a store. Let the sales team or manager know you're serious about a purchase by hanging around, toying with the merchandise. The more time a salesperson invests with you—hashing out details about different models, etc.—the more inclined he or she will be to close a sale.

Offer to pay in cash. Sweet music to some shopkeepers' ears, a cash offer can net you 5%–10% off the asking price. That's no sweat off a retailer's back, since credit card companies charge them a fee every time you pay with plastic—about 2%–5% for most purchases.

JUST SAY NO TO EXTENDED WARRANTIES

Don't blame a salesperson for peddling an extended warranty on items costing over $500. He or she probably pockets a generous commission from each costly contract sold. The value of such "warranties" to consumers, however, is far more dubious. For anywhere from $20 to $500 (or 10%–50% of an item's purchase price), these contracts promise to cover any repairs over a two- to five-year period. What you're buying, however, is really false security. The vast majority of new electronics and appliances will last for many years without a hitch. Faulty items that do go kaput tend to do so sooner rather than later, so your stan-

155

dard manufacturer's warranty—lasting for three months to two years—should suffice. Perhaps the best evidence of all that you can skip the extended warranty? Fully 80% of these contracts go unused.

TRY—OR OBSERVE BEFORE YOU BUY

Before you splurge on a big-ticket item, see if you can take it for a test drive of sorts. Many sellers are finding ways to let customers experience their wares in-store. Not only do you get a feel for an item, you're less likely to regret the purchase once you take it home. Most computer stores, for instance, let you run various software applications before you buy; and retailers such as Sears often display dishwashers and ovens hard at work, giving you a firsthand glimpse at their performance. One sporting goods store in Houston even lets shoppers strap on Rollerblades for a test skate around a 400-foot rink. If a product is not set up for an in-store trial, ask. You just may be able to give it a whirl.

SHOP WITH A PURPOSE TO AVOID IMPULSE BUYS

Are you in deliberate pursuit of a new stereo to replace an ancient phonograph? Or did you breeze by an audio store window display only to have your pulse rate quicken? Be warned about the latter scenario: such "impulse buys" can be the costliest purchases you'll ever make. With little forethought, that stereo may bust your monthly budget. Or worse, the high you got at the cash register store fades fast, and you rarely crank that CD player up at all. The next time you think, "I've got to have that," consider whether you would have put it on your shopping list earlier that same day. If the answer is no, allow yourself a 24-hour cooling-off period. You just might change your mind. After all, not buying is the best way to save.

SAVE BY DELAYING YOUR GRATIFICATION

That hot new model is here, it's arrived! You want it now, but the stores merely laugh at your bid to cut a deal. Can you do without it? Probably, at least for a while. And if you can sit still for six months, you're sure to score a lower price. This is especially true for electronics, where models are sometimes updated every six to 10 months.

Tips for Big-Ticket Merchandise, by Category

FURNITURE

Buying strategies: Furniture markups, as high as 300%, are among retailing's worst. Snaring a deal in local shops, outside sale dates, takes patience. Try asking to buy a floor model of a sofa or chair you like. Such a gently used piece will probably sell for half off. Also, consider going to auctions for character-hewn pieces. Check your local paper and Yellow Pages for auction houses, then pick up a catalog prior to attending. Smart shoppers can pay less than $100 for heirloom-quality furniture, like crystal lamps, framed mirrors, and oil paintings valued at far more.

Where to shop: Believe it or not, high prices for new furniture can merit an out-of-state shopping jaunt. Destination: High Point, North Carolina. The town is the nation's furniture Mecca, with over 60 discounters selling to the public. Prices on hundreds of manufacturers' goods run 30%–70% off regular retail. For more information, contact the High Point Convention and Visitors Bureau, 910-884-5255.

HOME ELECTRONICS

Buying strategy: For televisions, home videocameras, and major stereo purchases—anything over $750—make a bid that's $100–$200 below the asking price. Regardless of the price, you should at minimum get the store to forgive any delivery charges. Remember, you want costly, heavily used electronics to last for years. To ensure they'll stay humming, avoid the cheapest models, like that $200 VCR or that $159 color TV set.

Where to shop: Discounters such as Circuit City and Topp's offer some of the best buys. Or, to pick up fairly new, factory-serviced electronics (eschewed by their owners) try the Damark catalog (800-729-9000). Their products are in perfect working order, come with warranties, and cost about 20%–40% less than what you'd pay at a discounter's.

COMPUTERS

Buying strategy: Conduct some heavyweight comparison shopping, and then buy only as much machine as you need. Once you pick a model, be on the lookout for a store that offers a two-month price lock on any machine you buy. That way, if a model drops in price (as Apple computers did by 30% in late 1995), you get back the difference between the new low price and what you paid.

Where to shop: Competitive computer superstores like CompUSA and Computer City, and mail-order outfits such as USA Flex (800-777-2450) and MacWarehouse (800-255-6227).

JEWELRY

Buying strategy: Reserve your big bucks for items of true quality and endurance. Try to avoid paying a premium for brand names. A quartz watch, for instance, will do the trick whether it's a $30 Timex or a $4,000 Cartier Tank. Maybe you crave that Cartier for the sleek gold casing. That's fine, as long as you know that its quartz crystals are only a fraction more accurate than the Timex's. Similarly, a $10,000 Tiffany diamond probably gets about 30% of its value from the Tiffany name. Shop along New York City's diamond district, or any wholesale gem store, and you're sure to find comparable quality for a lot less.

Where to shop: Only at reputable jewelers you know or have been referred to by friends. Avoid buying fine jewelry at department stores. Their perpetual "sales" (GOLD 40% OFF!) indicate that the price was never fair in the first place; the mass-marketed pieces they stock tend to be low on quality and craftsmanship. When buying gems, seek an independent grading from the well-respected Gemologists' Institute of America (GIA). Certificates accompany all GIA-rated gems and are verifiable at GIA offices nationwide. Make sure fancy watches come in their original packaging, complete with written warranty and serial number—you don't want to pay thousands for a fake.

PINCHING TIP

Don't forget about trade-ins. Ask merchants if you can swap your used watch, jewels, furs, etc., for the newest item of your dreams. Just be sure you know the value of what you're giving up. That's the best way to know you've got a fair trade-in price.

FURS

Buying strategy: For the best savings on furs, shiver through the winter, then wrap yourself in mink and sable come March or April. Those are the months when retailers race to unload inventory, often shearing prices by up to 70%. Shop both furriers and department stores to get the best sense of pricing in your area. It also pays to be an informed shopper. For instance, does the fur get its rich color from nature, or is it dyed? Once you choose, ask the seller for a year's free storage. This perk, honored by many retailers, will come in handy for shoppers who heed our advice and buy late in the season.

Where to shop: Be sure to check out department stores, used-fur salons, and large furriers (such as Flemington). For Asia-bound travelers, amazing fur deals can also be found in Hong Kong's Kowloon shopping district.

APPLIANCES

Buying strategy: Generally, large appliances such as air conditioners and dishwashers carry a retail markup of about 15%. Smaller ones, like microwave ovens, are hiked up by 30%. Be sure to watch for energy efficiency. Manufacturers routinely place energy efficiency ratings on their products. Prices are higher on these items, but over the long term your energy savings should more than pay the difference—saving you money down the road. Keep in mind, however, that in order to be truly "energy efficient," an appliance should conserve power by about 30%–40%.

Where to shop: Discount appliance centers such as Circuit City, Tops, Sears, Montgomery Ward—even your local appliance dealer, who may be the most willing to cut you a sweet cash deal on certain products.

PINCHING TIP

Try a wholesale club for big-ticket purchases. Sure, you may already stock up on green beans and lightbulbs at places like Sam's Wholesale Club. But many of these places are now offering bigger, pricier items at rock-bottom prices. Good bets: jewelry, computers, and cameras.

SPORTING EQUIPMENT

Buying strategy: Serious equipment is a tricky buy. You want value, but not inferior quality. In fact, playing with inexpensive, poorly made gear may result in an injury. The best way to shop is to know your brands and troll for the best prices on specific items.

Where to shop: Watch for sales at stores with large selections, such as Champs and Sports Authority. One big discounter of golf and tennis equipment is Las Vegas Discount Golf & Tennis. The chain has over 70 stores nationwide and beats competitors' prices on high-end name brands such as Cobra, Prince, and Wilson. For a free catalog, call 800-933-7777 and ask to be put on the company's mailing list. (Also see box on pages 165–166.)

PRESCRIPTION EYEWEAR

Buying strategy: Shame that this should even be a "big-ticket" category. But if you care at all about looking stylish in your spectacles, you know that prices for a complete pair of glasses can easily exceed $500 and more in many cities. You can do better. Save 60% by shunning designer styles and opting instead for no-name frames made by the same manufacturer. Ask your optician to point these out. One example is the maker Luxottica, who produces high-priced lines for both Giorgio

Armani and Yves St. Laurent. The company's private label collection includes frames for under $100, or less than half
Armani's asking price.

If your prescription is low—say, you need glasses only for
reading—check out the selection of specs available at many
drugstores. Compared with your optometrist's offerings, they're
a steal at just $10–$25.

Where to shop: At your local optometrist, drugstore, or
department store.

When It Actually Pays
to Pay More

At the risk of blowing the entire premise of this book . . . it can
sometimes *pay* to overspend by 30% or more. How's that? In
rare cases a big purchase can qualify as an investment, and the
choice you make—depending on the item—can help you defer
replacements for years. Maybe the product has a history of
appreciating in value (such as a Rolex watch) or the manufacturer has a special guarantee on its products, saving you the
trouble of making costly repairs (Coach bags). Ask yourself if an
item satisfies any of the following criteria. Then let the guilt-
free buying begin.

IT STANDS TO LAST A DECADE OR MORE

Longevity is the most common reason to open your wallet
wide, especially for items you'll use every day. You can easily
justify buying a high-end mattress, such as a Serta Perfect
Sleeper or a top-of-the-line Stearns & Foster, since they are
known to last for 20 years or more.

IT CARRIES A LIFETIME GUARANTEE

That's a heck of a claim for any company, and one worth noting at the cash register—particularly if the product is timeless, like a classic handbag or a sturdy set of cooking pots. A few examples: Coach leatherware will replace or repair stitching, locks, and bindings for free as long as you own their bags (average price: about $250); All-Clad pots may cost double the price of their competitors' offerings, but for $350–$500 per set, you get superb aluminum and stainless-steel construction and a lifetime warranty. Keep in mind, however, that a "lifetime guarantee" is only as good as the company that issues it. So be sure to look for names that have been around for years.

IT'S MILES ABOVE THE COMPETITION

If you crave an item that works better than anything else like it, paying more shouldn't hurt too much. In fact, performance may be your top criterion for certain purchases anyway, like serious sporting equipment (for mountain climbing or skiing). In many cases the better the product, the less likely you are to sustain an injury.

IT COMES WITH STERLING SERVICE

Maybe you're trying to decide between items at two stores, but the price is 10% higher at one. It may well be worth the premium if one store goes the extra mile, giving great sales service, free delivery, or home installation.

CONVENIENCE OUTWEIGHS ALL ELSE

Saving big money on a last-minute purchase can be tough, and it may not be worth the hassle or time. Maybe you need a great-looking suit for a last-minute interview. You probably won't have hours to go mucking through sale racks. Likewise if you're jetting off to see a sick relative: you may have to shell out full price for an airline ticket. This is the price you pay for convenience, so don't sweat it.

SHOULD YOU FIX IT OR TOSS IT?

That stalwart TV has finally given out; or maybe the VCR's gobbling up videotapes. You've heard all about scams on electronics repairs, so should you fix it or cut your losses and buy a new gadget? Start with this fact: Just an estimate on home entertainment machines costs between $25 and $80. If you go ahead with the work, that sum gets credited toward the bill. To help cut your losses, consider these guidelines.

Television sets. These days a new television should last for about a dozen years. If your set is older than that and goes on the fritz, its complications are probably too costly to fix. Chuck it and start anew. Should your newer TV go grainy or produce an out-of-focus picture, consider what it cost. Those worn-out transformers, transistors, and resistors will likely run $75–$150 to replace. If you can get a new, similar set for $200 or so, you're better off.

VCRs. Some VCRs endure for up to 15 years, but you'll be lucky to watch videos problem-free for more than six. Problems are likely to afflict the belt or motor assembly and will cost $90 to $130 to cure. Cut your losses and toss it if the bill is more than that or if you've watched your six years' worth of bad movies.

Camcorders. Lug around a camcorder to the beach, family outings, and Junior's graduation, and what do you get? Troubles costing upward of $200, that's what. The good news

---

is that these machines are sturdy, even though their motors need cleaning after every 1,000 hours of shooting. Best to eat the repair costs on these zoom-and-pan jobs, since they can cost $1,000 or more to replace.

Answering machines. You'd be better off trying to fix Social Security than trying to repair the ills of an answering machine. Because they are relatively inexpensive anyway, there's no good reason to shell out big bucks for replacement costs here. Sustain your machine's life by selecting one with the longest possible warranty. Once that expires try again, or—hello, voice mail.

GET BIG-TICKET STUFF DELIVERED TO YOUR BOX

Shop till you drop, then consult a catalog. In some cases, you'll find, the best price is just a phone call away. Try these specialty sellers, who offer mail discounts of up to 60%. Most have catalogs, and all will quote the latest prices by phone.

- **For shutterbugs,** Porter's Camera Store, Inc., sells cameras, lenses, and other photographic equipment for 35% off list prices. Call 319-268-0104 for a free catalog.
- **Sporting types** will appreciate the following sources:
  1. Holabird Sports, for racket enthusiasts (410-687-6400), is where big names like Prince, Wilson, and Head rule, at about 20% off retail.
  2. Golf Haus is for serious swingers, selling deeply discounted (60% off some brands) bags, clubs, and other doffer supplies. All the biggest brands are here. Phone 517-482-8842 for a free price list.
  3. Bike Nashbar saves Tour de France wanna-be's as much as 30% on bikes, cycling clothing, and gear. Phone 800-NASHBAR for a free catalog.
- **Jewelry junkies** will love two well-respected mail-order discounters. The first is Albert S. Smyth, which promises discounts as high as 50% on high-end watches (like Omega and Movado), as well as on pearls, diamonds, and fancy pens. Dial 800-638-3333 for a free catalog. Brilliant savings can also be found in the pages of Michael C. Fina Co.'s catalog

(212-869-5050). It features a wide variety of cut-rate gold, diamonds, and precious-stone jewelry. Discounts go as high as 60%.

- **Techies** should check out Bernie's Discount Center, where all sorts of appliances and electronics choke the rafters. The New York City store offers a $1 catalog (refunded with purchase). Phone 212-564-8758.
- **For Web-heads,** there's the Computer Discount Warehouse, whose free catalog is crammed with famous brands like NEC, IBM, and Acer. Savings can log in at 50%. Call 800-800-4293.

CHAPTER 10

Building a Wardrobe without Busting Your Budget

You don't have to be a shopaholic or a clotheshorse to appreciate wardrobe savings these days. A few trips to Barneys New York (and other stores with prices to make you faint) should do the trick. We will concede, however, that shopping for clothes, shoes, and other closet conceits is an acquired skill: the more you do it, the more you learn and save. *Über*-shoppers can walk into a store blindfolded and identify cashmere spun from Mongolian goats—for 70% off. Less practiced types swear that a polyester suit feels like Savile Row wool and will snap it up, confident they've nailed a bargain.

But exactly what is a bargain? Frankly, it's all in the eye of the beholder, since appearances in the nation's $152 billion apparel business can easily deceive. "Sales" are now a daily event at most stores, which routinely mark up clothes 50%–100% from their wholesale cost. As any serial shopper can attest, then, *you probably haven't found an awesome bargain unless you've knocked 50% off the original asking price.* We can help.

Where to Shop

You want the best threads money can buy. That's not an assumption; it's a rule. There's a difference, you see, between *cheap clothing* and *clothing you buy on the cheap*. The former is rarely worth the money, since poor materials and fabrication don't last. Rather, it's the second sort that we're hoping to help you hunt down—and you may be surprised to learn where you will and won't find it.

• **Troll for designer deals at department stores but watch those "private label" sales.** Facing keen competition from off-price stores—not to mention general consumer malaise—once smug department stores are humbling their prices. Back in the free-spending '80s, upscale chains like Neiman-Marcus and Saks Fifth Avenue sold about half their merchandise at discount. What a difference a decade makes: *these days the bulk of department store goods—as much as 75%—flies out the door marked "sale."* As a general rule, the higher the sales ticket, the deeper the discounts are likely to go—sometimes as early as 10 weeks after merchandise arrives in stores. Most stores begin markdowns in earnest at the end of a season, making the weeks after Christmas and Labor Day prime sale dates. Swanky franchises may trim prices sooner, since stale merchandise only mars their *haute* reputations. Better to get those $375 pumps off the floor, goes the logic, even if it means marking them down to $79.

Now, in case you feel a tad guilty as the beneficiary of such spoils . . . don't. The stores can make big profits elsewhere, specifically on their so-called private label goods. Here's where to watch your step. Brands such as Macy's Charter Club and Nordstrom's Evergreen sport frequent sales tags for a reason: they carry the biggest markups in the joint. So while 30% off might sound like a nice price, it's still likely to be chump change. Instead, *you'll probably need to score a markdown of about*

168

50% to get a real private label deal. By the way, private label goods aren't necessarily unique to any one store, making price variations from one place to the next quite possible.

- **Off-price stores.** Not to be confused with outlets (see pages 170–171), off-price stores specialize in misfit merchandise in several categories: items may be slightly imperfect, discontinued, unsold from seasons past, or simply left over from a manufacturer's current stock (overruns). The savings—up to 80% off original prices—isn't without its hassles, as these stores demand patience, time, and flexibility. Colors and sizes tend to be limited, matchups with tops or bottoms are near impossible, and try-ons may not be permitted (only returns). Persistent digging, however, is sure to yield at least a few gems. Popular off-price sellers include Marshall's, Loehmann's, T. J. Maxx, Burlington Coat Factory, and Nordstrom's The Rack.

- **Consignment shops.** Calvin Klein and Geoffrey Beene may wince at the thought, but label lovers can pick up gently used designer clothing for 60% to 70% off original prices at upscale consignment shops. Popular in cities like New York, Boston, Dallas, and Palm Beach, Florida, these boutiques carry quality castoffs from society mavens and business types. Mrs. About Town, for instance, might send her twice-worn frocks to a consignment boutique, which pays her a commission when the garments sell. Such finds can round out a wardrobe nicely—especially if you're lucky enough to hit a shop with a donor who shares your measurements. When shopping in these stores, be careful to look for rips, stains, and other flaws before purchasing any garment.

- **Check out the brands at big discounters like Sears and Wal-Mart.** Relax. We're not hyping those Jaclyn Smith–inspired togs at Wal-Mart. The real bounty at big discounters is the basic, brand-name stuff. Don't overlook Sears,

Wal-Mart, and BJ's Price Club for famous label underwear, hosiery, and the like. Everyday discounts top 50%.

• **If you visit New York, go to sample sales.** When in New York, serious shoppers may want to hit a sample sale or two. Attracting a near religious crowd, these showroom sales let you pick from a designer's sample and overstock merchandise. Most prices hover around wholesale (again, that's 50% off retail to you and me), and amazingly, much of it is from current collections.

Designers big and small hold sample sales, so it pays to know who does so and when. Donna Karan, for instance, holds a giant sale twice a year, with roughly 50% off retail prices on clothing and accessories for both men and women. Other big sales worth noting are held by TSE Cashmere, Philippe Adec/Equipment, and Burberry. The most comprehensive guide to sample sales is the *S&B Report,* which carries 50–200 sale listings each month. An annual subscription costs $49 per year; or you can order a single copy for $9.95 by calling 212-683-7612.

PINCHING TIP

Women might try shopping in the boys' department of their favorite stores. If you're size 12 or under, you may spot deals (like designer shirts and accessories) for half the price of similar items in the women's department.

• **Don't be fooled by outlet malls.** Trust us—outlet deals are *dead.* The number of "manufacturer outlet stores" has more than doubled since 1990, to over 12,000 today, but their prices are rarely worth the trip. Formerly far-off warehouses stocked to the no-frills rafters, outlets today are likely to be housed in megamalls. Unfortunately these meccas are more of a boon to real estate developers than to customers like you. Because many outlets carry lines made especially for them (that's right, you may not find that dress or those shoes in any retail store), it's hard to know just how much you're saving. Even when outlets do carry top-of-the-line merchandise, pricing is spotty.

Three recent visits to outlet centers in Santa Fe, New Mexico, Birch Run, Michigan, and Secaucus, New Jersey, confirm this. Goods were picked over, much of it seasons old. As for prices? Imagine our surprise at finding a shirt at the J. Crew Outlet in Birch Run, Michigan, for $26 when we'd spotted the same item at a J. Crew store, on sale, for $7 four months earlier.

• **The outlet exception.** Alas, there's one way to wring value from the outlets: try calling ahead. Say you spy a swanky Calvin Klein coat at a department store, but the full price is high. Jot down the style number (found on the hang tag), and make a call to the designer's outlet nearest you. Believe it or not, outlet personnel will often field phone requests, telling you if they have the item in stock; they might even ship it for a nominal fee. One firsthand coup: a Calvin Klein nylon handbag, going for $500 at a New York City department store; a quick call to the Secaucus, New Jersey, outlet netted a sale price quote of $150—done deal.

13 Shopping Strategies That Can Cut Your Wardrobe Costs Down to Size

• **Keep tabs on two or three stores.** Few folks have the energy to vet every clothing sale. At the same time, it's distressing to miss out on "the big one." Could you have bought that top two weeks later for less? Did another store carry the same item for a deeper discount? Here's where you can take a tip from investors by sticking to what you know. Rather than careen from store to store in search of the holy grail of sales, settle on just two stores you really like. Then follow them as you would a stock. Get to know the salespeople; clip their coupons in the newspaper, and take note of how they mark down merchandise (reductions of 20%, then 50%, then 70%, for instance). Going for the broadest range of bargains, you might take a "high, low" approach—keeping tabs on, say, one department store and one off-price seller. Doing so should help you snag the merchandise you want at the right time.

• **If you buy at full price (gulp), watch for subsequent markdowns.** It happens. You go out on a limb to buy an item at full sticker or close to it, and bam! It heads to the 30% off rack just two days after your purchase. When that happens, ask a store manager to make an adjustment on your skirt or suit. You may be surprised to find how many stores will oblige. (Some salesclerks will even wink for you to come back in a week to claim a partial refund.) If you're refused a credit on a purchase of more than $100, you might consider returning the item, then buying it again—at the lower price.

• **Take advantage of department store credit discounts.** It's hard to rationalize department store credit cards, as most carry perilous interest rates, often topping 21%. One exception: when the issuing store gives you a discount—typically 10%–15% on any charges you make when opening up the account. That's worth considering if you plan to buy a whole wardrobe or think you will drop several hundreds of dollars in one spree. However, once you've done the discount charging deed, think twice about keeping the card—unless, that is, you've got the discipline to clear your balances each month.

• **Negotiate prices with managers.** Believe it or not, you may find success in haggling with apparel shopkeepers, even those working at large department stores. Garments that are slightly soiled, or have a few missing buttons, are ripe for a manager's impromptu markdown—if you ask. Sale items, too, may yield you a few dollars off the ticket. Is it the last of a bunch? Is it a hard-to-fit size? Is it an orphan jacket with no skirt or pants left to match? All are solid reasons to ask for a further reduction. Just make sure you speak with the department manager, not the cashier or salesclerk.

• **Check out a store's return policy, and keep your receipts.** What happens if you aren't satisfied with your purchase? Some stores will let you return clothing and accessories for cash or will post a credit to your charge account. Smaller boutiques and custom shops, however, often issue "store credit only"—a real bummer, since you've tied up your cash in a place that may not have a single item you want. It's worth noting the house rules before you buy a particularly costly item, such as a suit or a custom-made pair of shoes. Generally speaking, department stores have the most liberal return policies. As long as you have a receipt, most will issue full cash or plastic credits without a fuss—even weeks or months after the purchase. Some stores will still oblige even in the absence of a sales slip (but keep all of yours, just in case).

• **Ask for free alterations.** It's just one of those unfair facts of life. In many stores men still get their alterations included in the price of their suits, while women get left holding the sewing bag themselves—even though they pay more for their clothes. Next time your new garment needs a nip or tuck, ask for free tailoring services. You can make an especially good case for hems and sleeve cuffs, since men routinely get those jobs for free. Ask to speak to a manager, and cite any other shops you know that provide basic alterations gratis. This is a reasonable request, since a pair of $400 Ralph Lauren pants are cut to fit a six-foot-tall woman, not the average five-foot-four-inch woman.

• **Don't binge on designers' secondary labels.** Many label hoarders think they're being frugal by opting for items from a designer's secondary line. These are lower-priced collections (two examples: Ralph Lauren's Ralph and Donna Karan's DKNY) that cost about half their first-string counterparts. Yes, you still get the name. But quality is another story. Cuts, fabrics, and styles may waver much more here than in the designer's costlier primary line. Some of this stuff, in fact, is barely a match for the less expensive quality fare found at places like the Gap, Banana Republic, and L. L. Bean. It would be a mistake to construct a wardrobe from a designer's lower-priced line, since sales often bring designers' better clothing down to comparative levels.

• **Find a good tailor.** A good tailor can save you money by performing tricky alterations and even copying garments (like that $2,000 Hugo Boss suit) at your request. How many times have you found a fabulous suit or dress—marked down to nothing—just one or two sizes too big? For about $50 or so, a tailor can snip it to a perfect fit, sparing you the cost of buying another at full price. Ask store managers, friends, and colleagues for referrals. Before giving a tailor big business, test them out with a few small jobs, such as hems and cuffs.

• **When you can, buy clothing in a tax-heaven state.** Several states, including New Jersey, levy no sales tax on clothing. That's sheer bliss, considering how shoppers in New York and Texas get starched for as much as 8.25%—or $83 on a $1,000 suit. We're not suggesting you force your shopping and travel in sync. But when it comes down to large purchases (that suit, fur, or winter coat), it can make sense to delay gratification if a city on your itinerary has a branch of your favorite store.

• **Ask for a cash discount in boutiques**. A time-honed negotiator's tactic, offering to pay in cash can make a shopkeeper swoon. Aside from easing their cash flow, the cold hard stuff spares them the usage fee that credit card companies levy—about 2%–5% for most purchases. Try negotiating a cash discount while you're still deciding on the merchandise (wink). Once you reach for your wallet, you're probably too late.

- **Avoid shopping for sport.** Glance down at your shoes, your pants, your briefcase. Chances are at least one of those items was an impulse buy. You weren't looking for it. You might not have needed it. And you certainly didn't save for it. To avoid springing major budget leaks, schedule two major shopping trips each year: one in the spring and one in the fall. Allot a specific sum to spend, then make a list of the items you most need, plus fillers like blouses to round out your existing wardrobe. Bring coupons you've culled and photos you've cut from magazines. Think of shopping as a serious, not a frivolous, activity— big money *is* at stake. With that in mind, don't shop when you are bored, depressed, or newly broken up.

- **Think quality and versatility.** What's the construction on a garment? How long is it likely to hang sharp in your closet? You shouldn't be so taken by a dress or suit that you neglect to *size up its future prospects.* A bit (5% or less) of nylon, for instance, may give body and longevity to a wool blazer. Lycra or spandex does the same for wools and cottons. Seasonless fabrics (such as lightweight wool and cashmere-silk blends) will allow you to get maximum wear out of your clothing. One fabric faux pas: falling for the bad good stuff, like a low-quality $50 cashmere sweater (you can tell the quality kind from its heft and coat) or thin, noncolorfast silk that may require dry cleaning.

You'll also want to *pay close attention to colors,* since a palette that mixes three to four flattering shades lets you pull together more outfits from fewer pieces. Finally, *don't size up a garment in isolation.* Picture your entire wardrobe (can that jacket coordinate with one or two pairs of pants?) and consider any other purchases it might require (a dress that needs a pair of matching shoes or a special bag).

PINCHING TIP

Don't get ripped off by misleading labels. Carefully inspect the suit tag that boasts "Styled in Italy." There's a good chance it was actually made someplace like Mexico or Uruguay—countries not exactly known for their tailoring. The same goes for aggressive "cashmere" labels. Come fall, many coats flaunt such stickers on the outside. Read the interior label to find the truth: 20% cashmere, 80% wool.

• **Read labels to save on dry-cleaning costs.** Just a decade ago, it seems, only the fancy stuff required a dry cleaner's care. Not so today, as the apparel industry churns out more and more synthetic garments with "Dry Clean Only" labels affixed. Be sure to read the manufacturer's label on garments before you buy, since dry-cleaning costs can add up quickly. When you absolutely must use a pro, skirt around gimmicks like "French cleaning." Translation: same service, more money.

THE MAN'S SEASONLESS WARDROBE FOR $1,040

This suitcase-size wardrobe racks up lots of mileage. Everything matches. Everything packs. Nothing's fussy. Prices assume designer merchandise sold at off-price store savings.

✔ One suit, Italian-made, single-breasted wool crepe, in charcoal gray ($500)
✔ One sport coat in a neutral color such as brown or khaki, or a small check pattern to match many other colors ($200)
✔ One pair of pants, olive or black, pleated ($80)
✔ Two dress shirts with snap-down collars for versatility ($120 for both)
✔ One knit top, a pullover, to wear with suit pants and pleated pants, in a wool/silk blend ($70)
✔ Two neckties, striped or subtle pattern ($70 for both)

THE WOMAN'S SEASONLESS WARDROBE
FOR $1,170

Seasonless clothes give you the best buys. Classic clothes give you the best looks. Colors and accessories can help you to reflect fashion trends. They also let you go from daytime to night without a complete change of clothes.

✔ One matte-jersey dress, in black or dark navy ($100)
✔ One lightweight wool crepe suit (with skirt or pants) in black, navy, or camel ($500)
✔ One silk blouse in white or ivory ($75)
✔ One man-tailored cotton shirt in a neutral color or stripe ($40).
✔ Slim pant, cuffed, in a tropical wool or wool crepe ($75)
✔ Merino wool or cashmere-blend sweater set, in a gold, melon, or other citrus color ($100)
✔ Long, dark-colored cardigan sweater in a silk, rayon, or wool knit ($80)
✔ Waist-level leather jacket in black ($200)

CHAPTER 11

Savvy Ways to Save on Remodeling Your Home/Home Office

Any newsstand, with its glossy array of home remodeling and decorating magazines, tells the story of how Americans love to tinker around the house. And the fact that we plaster, paint, and hammer to the tune of $120 billion suggests that happiness is truly in the details.

The headaches of remodeling aside, most homeowners will eventually take up at least a minor rehab—for pleasure or profit. Maybe you crave an affordable luxury, like walk-in closets; or you need to update a drab bathroom to help speed an impending sale. Before embracing any project, however, do yourself a favor by checking your motivation. If the spruce-up is strictly a matter of personal comfort, fine. You'll want to save where you can, but there's no need to bite nails over the job's eventual payback, should you sell. For renovations that you do consider investments (such as enhancing the place for future

179

sale), it does pay to project how much of your money you're likely to recoup upon selling.

To maximize your renovating efforts on a modest budget, here are a few things you'll want to do:

MIND THE MARKET TO SAVE 10%–20% ON REMODELING COSTS

When you buy or sell a house, timing certainly counts. Since the same market forces affecting home sales drive the costs of remodeling (that is, materials and labor), timing is crucial for upgrades, too. It is best to undertake any grand projects, then, when home sales are in the doldrums. Unlike a hot market, when prices and building materials soar, a flat selling environment yields good bids from anxious contractors. Assuming you can defer work until market conditions change, you can save about 10%–20% on most projects.

DON'T GO OVERBOARD (NO MATTER HOW MANY DOLLARS YOU PINCH)

On some level, everybody plays "Keep up with the Joneses." It would be a mistake, however, to consider jobs that will raise your home's value by more than 20% above the priciest place in your area. Once you do move, that gold-encrusted bathroom may seem dreadfully out of place in the neighborhood, making your house a tough sell.

CONSIDER DOING (SOME) JOBS YOURSELF

Maybe you lack the skills to replace a roof or an entire kitchen. But with labor costs accounting for a full 40% of most remodeling jobs, maybe you should try rolling up your sleeves. Homeowners can save thousands by performing simpler, labor-intensive jobs (like painting, tiling, and lighting installation) themselves. Don't let inexperience stop you. Home Depot, for one, offers free weekly how-to classes to ambitious customers. The lineup changes monthly—tiling classes are most popular—and the lessons are conveniently scheduled for evenings. Call your local Home Depot for dates and information.

For those lacking the time and self-discipline to tackle and finish an entire job, another way to pinch dollars is to *be your own demolition man.* Tearing down a kitchen or a bathroom can account for about a third of your labor costs. Save this money by ripping out tiles, shelves, and wallpaper yourself.

DO-IT-YOURSELF JOB DOS AND DON'TS

Which projects should you attack around the house? The simple answer is, anything that's very labor intensive and doesn't require much skill or training. You'll want to stay away from jobs involving expensive materials, since one or two missteps could cost you hundreds.

- Do try your own paint jobs. You'd pay a professional about $300, plus materials, to paint the average-size living room. By flexing your own brushes, you stand to save 70%.
- Do remove wallpaper yourself. The tools for this easy job are available at your hardware store. Since it's practically a pure labor project, you'll probably save 90% off the 50 cents per square foot charged by a paper-hanging pro.
- Don't, however, try hanging paper yourself unless you've taken a course that shows you how. You don't want to botch costly paper.
- Do install your own insulation. You'd pay a pro about $950 to install the pink stuff, with a third of that cost going to labor. Pick up your own insulation at discount stores (most comes with instructions), and save more than 50% on the job.
- Don't tackle hardwood floors. A refinishing job requires real skill. Novices can easily ruin floor surfaces and foul up stain jobs, so the 70% do-it-yourself savings generally doesn't pay.

SHOP SMART

Generally you'll find the widest variety of materials, and the best prices, at warehouse-style home centers such as Home Depot, Lowe's, and 84 Lumber. Their freeway-size aisles give a clue about their low costs. Because they buy in massive quantities, they can afford to outstrip smaller sellers' prices, typically by 15%–30%.

For those projects you can pull off easily, try an *all-in-one kit*. Widely available in the stores just mentioned, kits give you everything you need to complete a deck, fireplace, home safety device, or backyard lighting system yourself. Not only do you get the satisfaction of seeing your own work spring to life, you get to admire handsome savings, too. For instance, a contractor might charge $7,000 to erect a wooden deck. Buy a kit, and you're likely to pay half that sum (plus any building permits you must pay). Fireplaces, too, which cost $5,000 or more (for labor and materials), are yours to build with a kit. Total cost for a metal firebox these days: about $500.

Another way to save on home projects, short of hiring your uncle for a couple of beers, is to check out *alternate materials*. Depending on your project, ask a contractor or a salesclerk at your shopping venue to recommend any cost-saving substitutes. The idea here isn't to skimp on quality, but to make informed buying decisions that could save hundreds or thousands. For instance, backyard tinkerers might look at Sur-Flex, a recycled rubber product that's environmentally sound and affordable. Costing about 25% less than easy-to-crack concrete, it is best used as a resurfacing material on patios and garden paths. Similarly, vinyl exterior surfaces have become a cheaper but sturdy alternative to aluminum siding—at about half of the cost to boot.

Don't overlook energy-efficient materials that can save you money on heating, lighting, and insulation. For instance, thermal wallpaper adds a cozy layer of insulation to outside walls, and decorative insulated tiles do the same for ceilings.

Concrete floors conserve more energy than regular tile floors and can be dressed up with paints and dyes.

Finally, before you set foot in a store, ask whether you really need to buy costly materials at all. In some cases you can *save by sprucing up what you've got.* A good example here involves a minor kitchen rehab. Rather than install brand-new cabinets, you can save *up to 50% on the total cost of your project* by refinishing those existing doors and shelves. To complete the look, replace the old pulls with brass or nickel-plated knobs.

AVOID A RIP-OFF BY HIRING THE RIGHT CONTRACTOR

Choosing the right contractor can save you from many financial nightmares. Primarily, a reliable pro is more likely to finish your job on time and close to (if not dead on) budget. More important, though, a solid contractor shouldn't leave you feeling vulnerable that the job will never get done. And given how 90% of all new contractors fold after just five years on the job, there is a real possibility that your contractor—and your money—could walk away in midproject.

Start your search for a hiring contractor by getting references from friends and local architects. Then contact the Better Business Bureau to find out about any recent complaints lodged against the business. You'll probably want to get bids from several contractors in the area. Talk through the project with each to make sure you share the same vision, and ask to visit the homes where they have recently finished jobs. Now comes the hard part: hammering out a written contract. Generally this document should spell out the timing and costs involved with your project. To save money, *insist on a fixed price* for the job rather than a by-the-hour rate, and be sure to specify any special materials to be used or avoided (such as redwood vs. pine for the deck). Before any job begins, check to see that the contractor carries adequate liability and workmen's compensation insurance. These coverages protect you in the event that a member of the crew gets injured on the job.

The American Homeowners Foundation offers consumers a six-page model contractor's agreement that can be customized for most projects. To get a copy, write to the foundation at 6776 Little Falls Road., Arlington, Va. 22213-1213. The contract costs $7.95, plus $2 for shipping.

ZERO IN ON PROJECTS THAT STAND TO PAY YOU BACK

The right home improvements do more than increase the quality of life in your castle. They can also put money back in your pocket when you sell. Of course, some projects are more value added than others. Kitchens and bathrooms, for instance, consistently reward remodelers with big paybacks. Swimming pools, on the other hand, can leave homeowners swimming in red ink, since they're likely to pay just 50% upon a sale.

How Seven Popular Remodeling Projects Stand to Pay You Back

PROJECT	COST	PAYBACK
Minor Kitchen Remodeling	$8,014	98%
Bathroom Addition	$11,639	89%
Major Kitchen Remodeling	$23,243	85%
Bathroom Remodeling	$8,365	81%
Master Suite Addition	$35,560	82%
Deck Addition	$6,528	71%
Home Office in Spare Room	$7,709	58%

Source: "Cost vs. Value Report," *Remodeling* magazine

Looking Good All Over:
Money-Saving Decorating Tips

So you're not Martha Stewart. In fact, you could use a little help in choosing the perfect living room carpet and hanging the drapes just so. But do you dare utter the words "interior decorator" without checking your bank balance first? Contrary to what you might think, a decorator's services aren't only for the rich. Sometimes it actually pays to bring a trained eye on board—especially if you must assemble a home quickly or if you're planning to buy all of your furnishings at one time.

HOW A DECORATOR CAN HELP YOU SAVE

In Chapter 9 we noted that markups on furniture could be as high as 300% at some stores. Because interior decorators buy sofas, fabrics, and other supplies at wholesale cost, they pass along some of those savings to customers. Of course, you'll pay a fee for their expertise, generally equal to about 30% of the wholesale cost of any furniture you buy. Your net cost working with a decorator, then, could actually be less than what you'd pay to root through stores on your own.

For simple jobs, head to the personal shopping division at your favorite department store. Decorating experts are on hand at most of the biggies, such as Bloomingdale's and Dillard's. Charging about $300–$1,000 to help you with color coordination and furniture placement, the stores usually apply those fees toward any furniture purchase you make in the store.

If you want to go a bit further, really stocking your place from carpets to chandeliers, you probably want to hire savvy eyes to do your selecting and buying. To find an interior designer you'll bond with, call the American Society of Interior Designers worldwide referral service at 800-775-2743. Make

185

sure you understand their fees and charges (some, for instance, will charge for their time in transit), and by all means try to negotiate their rates down. You may be successful if you promise to flaunt his or her work to your friends who also have the need for a decorator.

ASK A DECORATOR TO WORK WITH WHAT YOU HAVE

Don't feel obligated to send a decorator off on a buying spree. Some of the most successful room overhauls, in fact, can be achieved by using what you've already got. Many designing pros will agree to come to your home to rework the living room or bedrooms. Rather than buy new sofas and carpets, they might suggest reupholstering a piece of furniture or buying small items, like colorful pillows and throws, to dress up a room. Best of all, you won't go broke with such a gentle make-over. Expect to pay an hourly rate of between $50 and $150 for such room fix-ups.

Paying for Your Home Upgrades

You've got the low-cost plan down, but maybe you've got the sort of money that jingles, not folds. Can you still afford to install the dream? Absolutely. But first, don't make the mistake of rushing into debt to beautify your home. Assuming you've got some ready cash on hand, small projects like painting and wallpapering hardly warrant a loan with steep interest costs— even if it is tax-deductible. This rule applies mainly to minor projects of $5,000 or less. More ambitious jobs, of course, may require a plan of action that includes loans.

The best bet by far is a *home-equity loan*. After appraising your home's current value, most lenders will permit you to borrow up to 80% of your equity (you can figure your equity by subtracting your mortgage balance from the home's present market value). Aside from reasonable rates, recently averaging about 10%, the sweetest part about these loans is their tax-favored treatment. Provided that the debt on your first two homes is $1.1 million or less, interest on home equity loans is fully tax-deductible, up to $100,000.

Used mainly for larger projects, a *home-equity line of credit* works basically like a straight home-equity loan. The only difference is that homeowners tap their credit lines by writing checks from a special account when necessary. These may be ideal for long-term jobs, since you won't pay interest on money you have yet to spend. Unlike a home-equity loan, which features fixed payments, a home-equity line note will fluctuate with your loan balance.

Outfitting Your Home Office on a Budget

Working from home sounds appealing, even quaint. Getting set up to do so, however, will doubtless be a pain. If you plan on joining the 15 million Americans who work from home—or even if you just want a once-a-week escape from your city office—the biggest priorities should be comfort and efficiency. And of course, cost.

FURNITURE

Home office furnishings aren't too different from the stuff in your living room and bedrooms in that prices and quality vary dramatically. You can rest your haunches on a $49 Ikea swivel desk chair, or pay more than $700 for an ergonomic powerseat. Here's where you don't want to err on the cheap side. Your desk, chair, and computer table are more than just function and design; they could affect your health. While the average furniture setup can cost $2,000 or more, you can cut your budget to about $1,000 and make out just fine without compromising quality or comfort.

The workstation. Assuming you've got the space, and that you use a computer, you'll probably want at least two desk surfaces. The first is for paper pushing and other tasks; the second supports your computer. For the first type, you can afford to be as wacky and creative as you like. It's the latter, that station where you'll be sitting at a keyboard, that demands you be more pragmatic about shopping. Why? A plain old desk usually won't do for marathon computing and typing. Wrist injuries, increasingly common with heavy computer use, simply demand an ergonomically correct desk setup, or one that helps your body adjust to the unusual stresses of sitting and typing throughout the day.

Neither, however, has to be a costly setup. One option is an all-in-one L-shaped workstation that allows you to change tasks with a swivel of the chair. You've probably seen plenty of these setups at furniture shops for hundreds or thousands of dollars. Pass them by. Most are cheap laminates and hardly worth the dough. Instead, walk the aisles at places like Ikea and Staples— Office Depot. You'll come across a wide selection of workstations in the $70–$200 range. Rubbermaid also has a line of neat steel-reinforced computer pieces that snap together. A real bargain, these workstation components cost between $45 and $170 and are available at places like Staples—Office Depot.

You might also luck upon a great desk unit at a *used-furniture store or warehouse*. These are fabulous trolling places for budget-minded types, and they are likely to have gently used pieces costing a fraction of their new prices.

Don't go too cheap on the chair. How many minutes, hours, and days have you lost to unproductivity, compliments of your creaky office chair? While you certainly don't want a chair that breaks your back or your bank, a deskbound job demands that you have a comfortable, ergonomically correct chair. This simply means that its back, seat, and arms are adjustable. Among the best-quality chairs are those made by Turnstone (800-547-7333), with prices from $300. For about $100 you can get a Cadillac-model used chair at an office furniture or office supply store. Consult your Yellow Pages for the names of stores.

Consider going custom for storage space. In this instance, don't assume that custom-made means expensive. In fact, having shelves and bookcases built to your own specifications can cost less than half of what you'd pay for something prefab in a store. Find a good carpenter in your area, and ask for a price quote (it helps to be specific about the types of materials you want to use). Filing cabinets are an easier matter and can be found readily at discount stores for $50–$100.

Lighting. The best and most affordable lighting for an office of any kind is natural sunlight. If you have the luxury of selecting from among several spots in your home, go for the one with the most direct light. Any setup, though, requires a good, focused task light for your desk. One good bet is Adesso's Wall Street lamp (about $80).

SAVE ON EQUIPMENT; DELETE COMPUTER HASSLES

Good news for homebound computer jockeys: the home office market (or SOHO, for small office, home office) accounts for about 40% of all computer sales, making your choices better than ever.

Buy a package to save money. Today, the cutthroat computer industry has set about packaging its offerings. The result is often a better deal for consumers. Prices and selections from computer manufacturers change at a lightning pace. Recently, however, buyers could find packages that combined computer peripherals, CD-ROM drives, speakers, and even fax-modems for receiving and sending computer documents.

You need not spend more than $1,600 to get a machine that provides all these features and more. One selection popular with home office users is COMPAQ's Presario. It's loaded with software, including Quicken, an accounting program that home office entrepreneurs should find useful.

Save on your printer. It's all in the eye of the beholder. Do you require crisp type or speed? Or is it cost, cost, cost that drives your buying decision? Printers come in three basic varieties: top-of-the-line laser jets, which deliver outstanding print quality; dot-matrix, which range from eye-straining pixel type to respectable type; and ink jet, which offers near laser jet quality for less money. Assuming speed and readability are priority, an ink jet is easiest on the wallet. Top manufacturers include Canon and Hewlett-Packard. Prices range from $229 to $450.

Try an "office in a box." Once you've got your computer installed, you'll set off a domino set of nettlesome tasks, like faxing, copying, scanning, and printing. For those tight on space and cash, one excellent solution is a multipurpose machine. These nifty workhorses perform each of the tasks above and cost less than half of what you'd spend on individual components. Economical on space, too, they command no more room than your standard laser printer. Several manufacturers, such as Hewlett-Packard, Canon, Brother, and Xerox, are churning out these products at reasonable prices of $500–$750.

Software. If you're buying a new computer, it will probably come bundled with most of the software you need. These may include word-processing and spreadsheet applications. Should you need more firepower, you'll save hundreds by selecting an integrated package that combines various applications. The best example is a package like Microsoft Works. Available for DOS machines ($50), it covers your basic word-processing and database needs. Mac users should check out ClarisWorks, which handles the same tasks for about $150.

INDEX